A TREATISE CONCERNING THE
PRINCIPLES OF HUMAN KNOWLEDGE

A

TREATISE

Concerning the

PRINCIPLES

OF

Human Knowledge

PART I

Wherein the chief Causes of Error and
Difficulty in the *Sciences,* with the Grounds
of *Skepticism, Atheism,* and *Irreligion,* are
inquir'd into

By *George Berkeley,* M.A. Fellow of
Trinity-College, Dublin.

Edited, with an introduction, by
Kenneth P. Winkler

HACKETT PUBLISHING COMPANY
Indianapolis / Cambridge

GEORGE BERKELEY: 1685–1753

A TREATISE CONCERNING THE PRINCIPLES OF HUMAN
  KNOWLEDGE was originally published in 1710

Copyright © 1982 by Hackett Publishing Company
All rights reserved
Printed in the United States of America
Please note that the *Treatise* has been reset for the fifth (June 1995) printing;
the pagination therefore differs from that of previous printings.

10 09 08 07 06   7 8 9 10 11 12

Cover design by Richard L. Listenberger
Interior design by Dan Kirklin
Typeset by AeroType, Inc.

For further information, please contact
  Hackett Publishing Company, Inc.
  P.O. Box 44937
  Indianapolis, Indiana 46244-0937

  www.hackettpublishing.com

Library of Congress Cataloging-in-Publication Data

Berkeley, George, 1685–1753.
  A treatise concerning the principles of human knowledge . . . .
  Bibliography: p.
  Includes index.
    1. Knowledge, Theory of.   2. Idealism.   I. Winkler, Kenneth,
1950–   . II. Title.
B1331.W56   1982   121   82–2876
ISBN 0-915145-40-5   AACR2
ISBN 0-915145-39-1 (pbk.)

ISBN-13: 978-0-915145-40-9 (cloth)
ISBN-13: 978-0-915145-39-3 (pbk.)

Contents

Analytical Table of Contents

A TREATISE CONCERNING
THE PRINCIPLES OF HUMAN KNOWLEDGE

Numbers refer to sections

Editor's Introduction

If a tree falls in the forest when there is no one around to hear it, does it make a sound? George Berkeley answers that if there is really no one around, then not only is there no sound, but there is no tree, and no forest. In *A Treatise Concerning the Principles of Human Knowledge* his surprising answer receives its fullest defense.

What we now call the *Principles* is actually only the first part of a book Berkeley once hoped would include at least two parts. Part II was supposed to be about ethics, freedom of the will, and the nature of God, but Berkeley lost the manuscript while traveling in Italy, and never found the time "to do so disagreeable a thing as writing twice on the same subject" (Letter to Johnson, *Works* II, p. 282).[1] In the part that survives he argues that physical objects depend for their existence on the mind (sections 1–33), defends this view against a series of philosophical and religious objections (sections 34–84), and examines its consequences for skepticism and atheism (sections 85–100), natural science (or "natural philosophy," as it was then called, sections 101–117), mathematics (sections 118–134), the human soul (sections 135–145), and belief in God (section 146 to the end). But he does not leap into all this right away. He begins instead with an important Introduction on "the nature and abuse of language."

1. Abstract ideas

To appreciate Berkeley's Introduction it is important to share his sense of mystery over the capacity of mind and language to refer to things in the world. This capacity is especially mysterious in the case of language, because the words we use to refer to things could be other than they are. There is nothing special about the word "chair," for example, that accounts for its ability to refer to chairs. *We* use the word, but speakers

---

1. Sources of quotations from Berkeley are cited in the text. Citations include an abbreviated title of the work, followed in most cases by a section, dialogue, or entry number. Where it is not clear from the context, passages from the Introduction to the *Principles* are identified by the word "Introduction." For quotations from the *Three Dialogues*, the First Draft of the Introduction to the *Principles*, and the correspondence with Johnson, I indicate volume and page number in the Luce and Jessop edition of Berkeley's *Works*. For the *Dialogues*, I also give the page number in Adams' edition. Details on works cited are in the chronology and bibliography.

of other languages use other words, and if every speaker of English
agreed to switch the roles of "table" and "chair" we would get along just
fine, referring to tables when we used the word "chair" and to chairs
when we used the word "table." The relations between words and the
things they signify are arbitrary or *conventional.* This doesn't mean that
at some time in the distant past people consciously and ceremonially
agreed to use words in a certain way; it simply means that we now have
the power to alter the relations between words and the world by adopt-
ing new conventions, new associations of word and object. Now consider
a thought-experiment of which Berkeley was very fond. Imagine someone alone in the world without language. He still has tables and chairs
and mountains and rivers, but he lacks the words to refer to them. Can
he think about them anyway? "Of course he can," runs the obvious
reply. "Thoughts, like words, have the capacity to refer to things, a
capacity they do not owe to language." But thoughts, unlike words, do
not seem to be conventional. It is easy to imagine using the word "table"
to refer to chairs, but can we imagine using the *thought* of a table to refer
to a chair? "Call up the thought of a table but think of a chair instead"
sounds like a contradiction, because to call up the thought of a table is,
inevitably, to think of a table rather than a chair. A child may wonder
what the word "table" means, but it is impossible to wonder what the
thought of a table means. If you don't already know the meaning of the
thought, it is impossible to have it. Thoughts, it seems, are not conven-
tionally appointed to their symbolic roles, but demand a certain interpretation by their very nature. John Locke (1632–1704), author of *An
Essay concerning Human Understanding,* a book Berkeley studied care-
fully as a student and young scholar, calls thoughts "ideas," and suggests that words depend on ideas for their ability to refer to things.
Locke believes that the primary and immediate significations of words,
aside from "particles" such as *is* and *is not* and "negative" words such as
barrenness, are ideas. Ideas in turn signify things, establishing mediate
or indirect relations between words and the world. Berkeley accepts
Locke's suggestion, at least in the case of most words, and goes on to ask
what it is about thoughts or ideas that enables them to refer to things in
such a direct and irresistible way:

> Consider the different manners wherein words represent ideas, &
> ideas things. There is no similitude or resemblance betwixt words &
> the ideas that are marked by them. Any name may be used indif-
> ferently for the sign of any idea, or any number of ideas, it not being

determin'd by any likeness to represent one more than another. But it is not so with ideas in respect of things, of which they are suppos'd to be the copies & images. They are not thought to represent them any otherwise, than as they resemble them. (First Draft of the Introduction to the *Principles, Works* II, p. 129)

Ideas, according to Berkeley, are images: they are non-arbitrary or natural symbols, forced to represent what they resemble. Words on the other hand are arbitrary symbols, and refer to things only because they are linked to ideas. The link between words and ideas explains not only the capacity of language for reference (what I shall call from now on the *intentionality* of language), but also the possibility of communication. I am able to understand what you say because your words excite ideas in my mind just like the ones that prompted you to speak.

The line of thought I have just reviewed was very attractive to Berkeley, though he eventually decided its application had to be severely limited, a decision I will explain in the following section. It will pay for the moment to follow the line of thought a little further, because it helps explain why Berkeley denies the possibility of a mental activity known as *abstraction*.

It is easy enough to see how the link between word and idea functions in the case of a proper name. The name "George Berkeley" refers to Berkeley because it is linked to the idea of Berkeley. This idea is an image, the kind of thing we would have in mind if we faced Berkeley, or gazed at a portrait of him, and it represents Berkeley rather than anyone else because it resembles him so closely. But what about the common noun "man"? It too refers to things, so it must, on the present line of thought, be associated with an idea or image. Which one though? It cannot be the idea of Berkeley or any other particular man, because they have already been assigned the role of referring to particular men. If ideas alone are to account for the intentionality of language, a word's reference must be determined entirely by its associated idea. As soon as we allow a single idea to represent a particular man on some occasions and man in general on others, we introduce a looseness of fit between ideas and the world, and it was only the promise of a tight fit that made ideas plausible candidates for explaining the intentionality of language in the first place. It therefore seems that the idea corresponding to "man" must be a new idea, one which represents every man without representing any man in particular. But it is not clear where the idea is supposed to come from. Ideas of particular men, by way of contrast, can always be derived from experience directly. We don't need to make a special effort to form the idea of Berkeley: if Berkeley confronts us the idea enters, whether we like it or not. But because our experience is always of particular men and never of manhood itself, the idea of man in general must be the product of some kind of mental manufacturing. Berkeley reports on the form the manufacturing allegedly takes in section 9 of the Introduction:

> For example, the mind having observed that *Peter, James,* and *John,* resemble each other, in certain common agreements of shape and other qualities, leaves out of the complex or compounded idea it has of *Peter, James,* and any other particular man, that which is peculiar to each, retaining only what is common to all; and so makes an abstract idea wherein all the particulars equally partake, abstracting entirely from and cutting off all those circumstances and differences, which might determine it to any particular existence.

Berkeley describes here the activity of separating or *abstracting* the quality of manhood from a collection of ideas of particular men. The product of the activity must, he thinks, be an image, but it will have to be an image of a very unusual kind. Because all men have both color and shape, the image of man in general must have color and shape as well, yet it cannot have a *particular* color or shape without endangering its role as the indifferent representative of all men. If the image, for example, were crooked and white, it would represent a crooked and white man rather than every man. But Berkeley argues that any image with color and shape must have a particular color and shape—a fact he thinks each of us can verify by introspection. Try to imagine something with color and shape but without any color or shape in particular: "The idea of man that I frame to myself," Berkeley says of his own attempt, "must be either of a white, or a black, or a tawny, a straight, or a crooked, a tall, or a low or a middle-sized man" (Introduction 10). Because there can be no abstract images, he concludes, there can be no abstract ideas.

Few philosophers have been convinced by Berkeley's argument. Some criticize him for assuming that an idea must be an image. He may be right about the determinacy of images, they say, but if the defenders of abstraction deny that ideas are images, his argument will simply be irrelevant. Others complain that even if ideas are images, Berkeley's failure to form an image of man in general is a personal one, displaying the limits of his own imagination but telling us nothing about the limits of the human imagination itself.

Berkeley has a reply to each of these objections; but more important, he has a second, deeper argument against abstraction, one which depends neither on the assumption that abstract ideas are images, nor on his failure to bring them into introspective focus. Consider, for example, the abstract idea of a triangle in general. The idea calls for the mental separation of triangularity–the complex of qualities all triangles share–from the inessential qualities some triangles have and others lack. Triangularity itself is what philosophers call a *universal*, a property capable of existing (or being exemplified) in many different places at the same time. No one doubts that triangularity exists, or at any rate "occurs," wherever triangles do; the interesting question is whether it is capable of existing by itself. Berkeley's answer is no. He claims that all "things"–and by "things" in this case he means all entities capable of independent existence–are "in their own nature *particular*" (Introduction 15). In *Three Dialogues* 1 he has his spokesman Philonous describe the maxim that *"every thing which exists, is particular"* as "universally received" (*Works* II, p. 192; Adams, p. 28), and there can be no doubt that when Philonous speaks, Berkeley is thinking of Locke–the only defender of abstraction Berkeley identifies in the *Principles*–who denies the separate existence of universals several times in his *Essay*.[2] Return now to the abstract idea of a triangle. To form the idea is to form an idea of triangularity and nothing else. Now suppose that the content of our thinking is determined by the idea we confront in thought. (This is closely related to the thesis, discussed above, that the reference of a word is determined entirely by its associated idea.) As soon as we make this assumption, we are apparently left with no way of distinguishing between *conceiving of nothing but triangularity* and *conceiving of the separate existence of triangularity*, since either content seems to call for the same idea. If so, it follows that in forming the idea of triangularity, we are conceiving of the separate existence of triangularity–conceiving, in other words, of the impossible. One of Berkeley's most deeply held beliefs is that conceivability and possibility coincide: a state of affairs is conceivable, he thinks, if and only if it is possible. He grants that we can abstract the smell of a rose from the flower itself, or the trunk of a human body from its limbs, but only because these things "may really exist or be actually perceived asunder" (*Principles* 5). Abstraction in what he regards as the strict sense–the mental separation of what cannot

---

2. See *Essay* III iii 1, 6, and 11. Berkeley refers to the passage from *Essay* III iii 6 at Introduction 11.

exist separately–is absolutely impossible: "My conceiving or imagining power," he says at *Principles* 5, "does not extend beyond the possibility of real existence or perception." Elsewhere he puts it this way:

> It is, I think, a receiv'd axiom that an impossibility cannot be conceiv'd. For what created intelligence will pretend to conceive, that which God cannot cause to be? Now it is on all hands agreed, that nothing abstract or general can be made really to exist, whence it should seem to follow, that it cannot have so much as an ideal existence in the understanding. (First Draft of the Introduction, *Works* II, p. 125)

Not even God, Berkeley thinks, can create an independently existing universal. And if it is beyond God's power, he asks, how can we even conceive of it, since God is certainly able to accomplish anything a finite being is able to imagine. Berkeley's confidence on this last point is not hard to appreciate: if we can conceive of it God can conceive of it too, but then given his omnipotence, what obstacle could there be to his bringing it about?

Berkeley's argument raises three important problems:

(1) It might be asked what right Berkeley has to say that God cannot create a separately existing universal. If God really is omnipotent he should be able to, but if he can, separately existing universals are possible, and Berkeley's argument collapses. The reply to this objection turns on Berkeley's understanding of impossibility. When Berkeley calls something impossible, he means that it is contradictory or inconsistent. In *Three Dialogues* 2, for example, Philonous asks Hylas when a thing is shown to be impossible, and Hylas answers, "When a repugnancy is demonstrated between the ideas comprehended in its definition" (*Works* II, p. 225; Adams, p. 60). In *Alciphron* VII 6 (first and second editions), Euphranor asks Alciphron what things are impossible. Alciphron answers "such as include a contradiction," and Euphranor then makes use of this reply in his own version of the argument against abstraction now before us. An example of an inconsistent or contradictory state of affairs is the existence of a married bachelor. Because a bachelor is unmarried by definition, the suggestion that a man might be a bachelor and married at one and the same time is inconsistent, and because it is inconsistent, not even God can bring a married bachelor into being. If God creates a bachelor, then by definition he creates a man who is unmarried, and if he creates a married man, then by the same definition he creates something other than a bachelor.

Berkeley thinks that separately existing universals, like married bachelors, are inconsistent. He therefore concludes that even God is powerless to create them. It is not as if God can conceive of a separately existing universal, but finds himself frustrated when he attempts to give what he conceives a worldly form. It is "impossible even for an infinite mind to reconcile contradictions" (*Principles* 129). God's powerlessness, then, is no threat to his omnipotence. An omnipotent being is not a being who can do anything at all, but a being who can do anything that can be done.

(2) The defense I have just provided succeeds only if the separate existence of universals really is contradictory or inconsistent. Can Berkeley prove that it is? We can see the magnitude of the problem he faces if we look more closely at the notion of a married bachelor. It is easy to show that the notion is inconsistent because the notion of a bachelor is itself complex. We can analyze *being a bachelor* into *being a man who is unmarried,* and since to call a man unmarried is to deny that he is married, "married bachelor" is a clear contradiction. But the idea of triangularity is different. It is derived from ideas of particular triangles, just as the idea of man in general is derived from ideas of particular men, and Berkeley's account of such derivation at Introduction 9 suggests that the idea of triangularity is *part* of every idea of a particular triangle. Yet the idea of any particular triangle must be consistent (otherwise the triangle would not exist), and if it is, how can we come up with an inconsistent idea simply by removing or abstracting a certain part of it? The possibility of contradiction or inconsistency seems to depend on opposition between elements in a complex ("repugnancy," as Hylas puts it, between ideas comprehended in a definition); but if the opposition is not there in the complex to begin with, it hardly seems possible to introduce it by simplification. Berkeley is aware of this problem but he has no solution to it. On the one hand, he wants to understand impossibility objectively. He doesn't want the claim that something is impossible to be nothing more than a report of the failure of some mind or other to conceive of it. He identifies impossibility with inconsistency because he wants the claim to tell us that *no one* – not even God – can conceive of it. On the other hand, his objective test of inconsistency – the analysis of complex notions into their constituent parts and the subsequent search for oppositions – does not allow him to prove that everything he wants to call impossible really is. Before we condemn him, though, we should recall that Locke himself agrees that universals cannot exist separately. It was, in fact, taken for granted by Berkeley's

contemporaries that abstraction involves the separation in thought of things that are inseparable in the world. John Norris (1657–1711), a friend and philosophical opponent of Locke, writes for example that "where things are really separate or distinct, the considering them apart is not *Abstraction*, but only a mere divided Consideration." He observes that "Abstraction is, as it were, the drawing of a thing away from itself."[3] (Compare these remarks to *Principles* 5, where Berkeley gives the same analysis of the proper meaning of abstraction, and says that he might as easily "divide a thing from itself" as abstract the being of a thing from its being perceived.) Even if Berkeley's argument fails to show that abstract ideas are absolutely impossible, then, it may succeed as an *ad hominem* argument against the defenders of abstraction (and Locke in particular), *ad hominem* ("to the man") not in the sense that it attacks a position by insulting the person who takes it up, but in the sense that it attacks the position of a concrete opponent, whose other commitments may rule the position out. Locke not only agrees that universals cannot exist separately; he also agrees that whatever is impossible is inconsistent, and that nothing inconsistent can be conceived.[4] There is, however, one premise in Berkeley's argument Locke does not seem to accept, and this brings us to our third and final problem.

(3) Locke may be able to escape Berkeley's argument by making a simple distinction. "It is true that I cannot conceive of the separate existence of triangularity," he may say, "but why suppose that I conceive of any such thing when I form the abstract idea of a triangle? There is a difference between conceiving of nothing but triangularity, and conceiving of its separate existence, and while the latter is impossible for the very reason you suggest, only the former is required by my doctrine of abstraction." Locke will be able to take advantage of this defense if he conceives of abstraction as selective attention. "When I conceive of nothing but triangularity," he can say, "the only ideas before my mind are perfectly ordinary ideas of particular triangles. They have all the complexity it takes to qualify as ideas of particular triangles, but I ignore all this and focus on their triangularity, the one quality they have

---

3. *An Essay towards the Theory of the Ideal or Intelligible World*, volume 2, p. 174.

4. For the inconsistency of the impossible (in the form of the equivalent claim that the consistent is possible) see *Essay* IV iii 6, where Locke says that his reason for thinking matter may think is that he sees no contradiction in it; for the inconceivability of the inconsistent, see *Essay* III x 33 (a passage Berkeley cites in section 125 of *A New Theory of Vision*).

xix

in common." To conceive of abstraction as selective attention is to deny what I call the *content assumption* – the assumption that the content of thought is determined by its object. On the view I am now suggesting might be Locke's, we may be thinking of a particular triangle or of triangularity in general while confronting one and the same idea, *depending on how much of the idea we attend to.* The content assumption is essential to Berkeley's argument, because only on that assumption can he move from the claim that we cannot conceive of the separate existence of triangularity (a claim entailed by those premises in the argument Locke himself accepts) to the conclusion that we cannot form the abstract idea of a triangle. If he denies the content assumption, Locke has no obligation to account for the abstract character of our thinking by pointing to a strangely abbreviated object of thought. He can grant that it is impossible to form an idea which, due to its internal features, represents nothing but triangularity, but he can add that this in no way detracts from our ability to attend selectively to our ideas. The burden would then be on Berkeley to prove that the distinction between conceiving of nothing but triangularity and conceiving of its separate existence cannot be maintained. But it is a distinction Berkeley accepts himself: "We may consider *Peter* so far forth as man, or so far forth as animal," he writes, "inasmuch as all that is perceived is not considered" – that is, inasmuch as all that an idea contains is not attended to (Introduction 16). Berkeley even appeals to our capacity for selective attention to explain how a geometrical proof involving the diagram of a particular triangle can nevertheless apply to any triangle whatsoever. He explains that the individuating features of the triangle in the diagram are not "concerned in the demonstration. . . . And here it must be acknowledged," he continues, "that a man may consider a figure merely as triangular. So far he may abstract" (Introduction 16).

While the text of Locke's *Essay* does not prove that he conceives of abstraction as selective attention, several scholars have argued convincingly that he does.[5] One point in favor of their interpretation is that Locke never endorses the content assumption. We have seen that Berkeley denies the content assumption, but attributes it to Locke. How can Berkeley make the attribution so confidently? The answer lies, I think, in Locke's use of the word "idea." Locke sometimes writes as if ideas determine the content of thought, but when he does, he is not thinking of ideas as the *objects* of thought – as entities we confront in the way we

---

5. A recent example is Mackie, *Problems from Locke,* pp. 107–12.

confront images and pains–but as the thoughts themselves. (On this interpretation of "idea," the claim that ideas determine the content of thought is true, but trivial.) At other times Locke writes as if ideas are objects, but then he tends *not* to suppose that they determine content. Berkeley is much more definite in his understanding of ideas: he thinks of them, unequivocally and unvaryingly, as images–a kind of object. So definite is his understanding that he cannot help but suppose it is also Locke's understanding. The result is that when Locke writes as if ideas determine content, Berkeley takes him to be saying that the *objects* of thought determine content, and therefore the possibility that Locke conceives of abstraction as selective attention never occurs to him. Berkeley then treats selective attention and the accompanying denial of the content assumption as his own philosophical discoveries, though they may well have been made (admittedly in a less clear form) by Locke himself.

Before we leave Berkeley's Introduction and turn to the *Principles* itself, we should take note of three things. (1) Berkeley's main argument against abstraction does not derive its strength from his belief that ideas are images. Anyone who makes the content assumption will have a difficult time explaining how we can conceive of a universal without conceiving of its separate existence–whether he thinks of ideas as images or not. And if we follow Berkeley's example and conceive of abstraction as selective attention, we can regard ideas as images without falling victim to the argument. In general, the belief that ideas are images has had an importance in the criticism of Berkeley that it does not deserve. Berkeley is often attacked for "assuming" that ideas are images by philosophers who have become convinced that thinking does not require an introspectible object of any kind. But Berkeley does not *assume* that ideas are images; he *concludes* it, as part of a conscious attempt to account for the intentionality of thought. At the same time he denies the content assumption, and so becomes one of the first philosophers to realize that the inner object, by itself, cannot explain why thought has the content that it does. (2) Our discussion in this section has been confined to only one of the two kinds of abstraction Berkeley criticizes. Besides the mental separation of general qualities, he also attacks the mental separation of specific qualities–determinate sizes, shapes, and shades of color–from qualities of other kinds with which they must occur. He describes this kind of abstraction in Introduction 7, and argues against it in 10. (3) At Introduction 13, Berkeley quotes Locke's own description of the general idea of a triangle. Locke writes that the idea (or the triangle that it represents – the subject of the description is unclear) "must be neither Oblique, nor Rectangle, neither Equilateral, Equicrural, nor Scalenon; but all and none of these at once. In effect, it is something imperfect, that cannot exist; an *Idea* wherein some parts of several different and inconsistent *Ideas* are put together" (*Essay* IV vii 9). It is possible to take this description as a confession that the idea is an inconsistent complex of opposing elements. Berkeley has been criticized for taking it this way, and for failing to see that all Locke intends to say is that the idea represents every triangle without representing any triangle in particular. But this criticism is unfair; Berkeley reads Locke's description as generously as anyone.[6] When he pokes fun at Locke's description or fastens on Locke's use of the word "inconsistent," it is not because he thinks Locke acknowledges the inconsistency, but because he has an argument that Locke *must* acknowledge it.

2. Immaterialism

Philosophers of the seventeenth and eighteenth centuries typically describe the world in terms of the independently existing things, or *substances*, that inhabit it. Berkeley argues that the only substances are minds or spirits, and that anything else we are prone to regard as a substance – a house, a mountain, or a river, "in a word," any of "those bodies which compose the mighty frame of the world" (*Principles* 6) – is not a substance at all, but a collection of ideas which depends for its existence on the mind. Berkeley thinks there are no *material* substances at all. This *immaterialism* or *idealism* is best understood in terms of the materialist view of the world to which Berkeley opposes it. The materialist world-view has four main elements:

(a) *Physical objects would survive even if there were no minds.*

(b) *Physical objects cause ideas to arise in our minds.*

6. Proof is provided by *Alciphron* VII 5 (in the first two editions) and *A Defence of Free-thinking in Mathematics* 45–47. In both places Berkeley presents a close paraphrase of Locke's description, and follows it with a description very much like the ones he himself gives at Introduction 8 and 9. Each time he makes it clear that the two kinds of description come to the same thing. This explains why he does not think he is introducing a third kind of abstract idea when he quotes Locke: the two "proper acceptations" of abstraction have already been introduced by section 10. *Defence* 45 is especially instructive because it shows that Berkeley takes Locke to say it is the general triangle, rather than the general idea of a triangle, which is "something imperfect, that cannot exist."

(c) *Physical objects have two kinds of qualities,* primary *and* secondary. Every physical object is a system of insensible particles, tiny pieces of matter too small to be seen or felt. Considered in themselves these particles or atoms have only *primary* qualities, the qualities scientists tell us they have: solidity, extension, figure, motion or rest, and number. (The list is Locke's, *Essay* II viii 9.) These qualities give objects the power to produce ideas of *secondary* qualities (colors, tastes, smells, and so on) in perceiving minds, but there is nothing resembling those ideas in the objects themselves. "If a tree falls in the forest when there is no one around to hear it, does it make a sound?" The answer depends on how sound is understood. If the question is whether the tree produces an *idea* of sound, the answer of course is no, because ideas cannot exist outside of minds. If the question is whether the tree or surrounding air has the *power,* when there is a normal perceiver in the vicinity, to *produce* an idea of sound, the answer is yes. If the question is whether there is something in the tree resembling the idea of sound, the answer is no – but in this respect, unperceived falling trees do not differ from perceived ones. There is nothing inside *any* physical object that resembles an idea of sound. There is the idea in the mind of the perceiver, the power in the object to produce the idea (a power the object owes to the arrangement of particles within it), and that is all.

(d) *It is impossible to* prove *that the physical world exists.* If anyone is stubborn or perverse enough to deny the existence of the physical world, there is no way to prove him wrong. All that we immediately perceive are our own ideas, and they give no guarantee that a world lies beyond them. For all we *know* (if to know something is to be certain of it), we might be living through an elaborate and powerfully convincing dream. But despite its irrefutability, skepticism about the physical world is not worth taking seriously.

I shall discuss Berkeley's reaction to each of these elements in turn.

(a) *Physical objects would survive even if there were no minds.* Berkeley's argument against the first element in the materialist world-view is astonishingly brief. He points out (*Principles* 4) that (1) we perceive physical objects, and (2) we perceive only our own ideas. It follows that physical objects must *be* ideas, for if they were not, we could not perceive them. But ideas depend for their existence on the mind, and exist only as long as they are perceived. Therefore the same must be true of physical objects.

At first glance Berkeley's case seems to rest on a simple mistake. According to the materialist world-view, the word "perceive" is ambiguous, because perception can be either *immediate* (direct) or *mediate* (indirect). All that we *immediately* perceive are our own ideas, but on the materialist account of experience, immediate perception of an idea amounts to mediate perception of a thing. Thus the first premise of Berkeley's argument is true only if we understand "perceive" as "perceive mediately," while the second is true only if we understand it as "perceive immediately." Since this crucial word has a different sense in each premise, it is impossible to draw a conclusion.

Though the opening sections of the *Principles* conceal it, Berkeley is aware of this objection. He responds to it in later sections by criticizing the notion of mediate or indirect perception. Perceptions, like ideas in general, have the capacity to refer to things (they are, like words, *intentional*), and Berkeley thinks this capacity can be explained only if there is a non-arbitrary, non-conventional relation between perceptions and the world. He believes there are only two candidates for this relation—resemblance and cause and effect—and he argues that neither is available to the materialist.

There can be no relation of resemblance between ideas and things because "an idea can be like nothing but an idea" (*Principles* 8). Unfortunately, Berkeley's published defense of this "likeness principle" neglects the very distinction between direct and indirect perception which the principle is designed to upset:

> I ask whether those supposed originals or external things, of which our ideas are the pictures or representations, be themselves perceivable or no? If they are, then they are ideas, and we have gained our point; but if you say they are not, I appeal to anyone whether it be sense, to assert a color is like something which is invisible; hard or soft, like something which is intangible; and so of the rest. (*Principles* 8)

The point of the distinction between direct and indirect perception is that we cannot conclude that objects are ideas simply because objects are in some sense perceived. Objects are perceived indirectly, and while this distinguishes them from ideas, it does not make them invisible or intangible. It follows only that they are not visible or tangible *directly*. Berkeley gives a better defense of the likeness principle in his notebooks, a defense he hints at in *Principles* 8 when he writes that "if we look but ever so little into our thoughts, we shall find it impossible for us to conceive a likeness except only between our ideas." The defense is that because we immediately perceive only our own ideas, it is impossible to compare an idea to a thing. And if it is impossible to compare them, the defense continues, it makes no sense to suggest they are alike. The materialist might reply that in fact we *can* compare them; it is just that when we do, we are forced to consult the thing through our idea of it. But it seems that any genuine attempt at comparison must have as a possible outcome the judgment that the things compared are not alike, and if all we do is compare the idea to itself–because the idea provides our only access to the thing–that outcome is ruled out from the very start. Still, the materialist might maintain that an idea can resemble a thing even if we are unable to verify it. The basic issue is whether we can have a conception of a state of affairs when we have no means, even in principle, of finding out that it obtains. The materialist thinks we can; Berkeley thinks we cannot. The basic issue still divides philosophers today. Berkeley may be wrong about it, but it remains true that the materialist has no way of *knowing* that the resemblance he posits is really there.

Even if the relation of resemblance were available to the materialist, his account of the intentionality of perception would probably appeal to cause and effect as well. Resemblance between an idea and a thing, after all, does not guarantee that we are perceiving the thing rather than imagining it. What distinguishes imagination from perception is that in perception, the idea is caused by the object's presence. Berkeley argues, though, that a thing is no more capable of causing an idea than it is capable of resembling it. For Berkeley, the notion of cause and effect is closely linked with that of understanding. To identify the cause of an event, he thinks, is to convey an understanding of *why* the event occurred. It is to make the event intelligible. It is not enough to point to an event that habitually precedes the event to be explained; we may have observed the sequence a thousand times, but if we have no insight into the manner in which the alleged cause operates, we have no right to speak of it as a cause at all. Berkeley's objection to a cause-and-effect relation between things and ideas is that no one, not even the defender of material substance, pretends to understand how the action of matter on mind can produce ideas. And if we cannot understand it, he insists, we cannot legitimately regard things as the causes of our ideas.

Because neither resemblance nor cause and effect is available to support it, Berkeley concludes that the materialist's distinction between direct and indirect perception is mistaken. Apparently the notion of perception is not ambiguous after all, and Berkeley's immaterialist conclusion is safely established. The materialist, of course, may try to rehabilitate his position by revising his conception of a physical object. Berkeley's immaterialist argument purports to show that perceived qualities cannot exist in matter, because perceived qualities are ideas, and ideas cannot exist in a thoughtless thing. But perhaps there are material substances with qualities we cannot perceive, qualities "as incomprehensible to us as colors are to a man born blind" (*Principles* 77). Berkeley's reply to this is that he sees no point "in disputing about we know not *what*, and we know not *why*" (*Principles* 77). If the materialist retreats to the position that matter is an "unknown *somewhat*, neither substance nor accident, spirit nor idea, inert, thoughtless, indivisible, immoveable, unextended, existing in no place," Berkeley observes that this is just to use the word "matter" as everyone else uses "nothing" (*Principles* 80). The notion of matter, Berkeley argues, is contradictory or empty: contradictory if matter is taken to be the substratum of perceived qualities, which because they are ideas can exist only in a mind; empty if taken to be the substratum, in a sense unexplained, of qualities unknown.

Berkeley, incidentally, does not reject the traditional view that qualities cannot exist apart from a substance or substratum. Though he deprives perceived qualities of a material substratum, he gives them a place in a spiritual substratum or mind. One advantage of placing them there is that it enables him to give a non-figurative account of what it is for a quality to exist or inhere in a substance: inherence (being-in) is being perceived. He does depart from tradition, though, on a related point. On the traditional view, a quality inhering in a thing can also be attributed to the thing. If the color white, for example, exists in a substance, then the substance can be called white. But Berkeley does not want to say that the mind is white or extended, even though color and extension exist in it. They are in the mind "not by way of *mode* or *attribute*, but only by way of *idea*" (*Principles* 49). It might be objected that it was only the fact that qualities are attributes of things that made them look like dependent entities in the first place. If we follow Berkeley and separate inherence and attribution, the objection continues, we will no longer be able to base the metaphysical distinction between independent substances and dependent qualities on the grammatical distinction between subject and attribute. Berkeley would reply, I think, that language should never be taken as a guide to metaphysics. Language can mislead us (it suggests, for example, that every grammatical subject picks out an independent substance), but we cannot be misled by the obvious dependence of ideas on minds or spirits.[7]

(b) *Physical objects cause ideas to arise in our minds.* We have seen that physical objects as the materialist conceives of them cannot be the cause of our ideas. But if we conceive of physical objects in the way Berkeley favors, as clusters of qualities dependent on the mind (as clusters, in other words, of ideas), Berkeley argues that they cannot qualify as the cause of anything. The reason is that ideas contain nothing but what is perceived. They are transparent, he thinks; nothing in them is hidden from view. And if we look closely at our ideas, we "will not perceive in them any power or activity" (*Principles* 25). It follows that qualities and clusters of qualities are causally inert. Because neither matter nor perceived qualities can be the cause of our ideas, Berkeley looks to the only remaining candidate–mind or spirit.

As we have seen, Berkeley demands that causal explanations meet a very high standard, and it is a mistake to associate him on this point with David Hume (1711-1776), whose standards were much more re-laxed. It was Hume who argued that there is no necessary connection between cause and effect, and in this he may well have been influenced by Berkeley's observation that there is no necessary connection between a natural event and what is ordinarily regarded as its cause. But the point behind Berkeley's observation is that what we ordinarily regard as causes are not really causes at all, but are instead mere marks or signs of what is to follow, giving us "a sort of foresight, which enables us to regulate our actions for the benefit of life," and yielding no insight into why things happen as they do (*Principles* 31). It is precisely because he insists on a necessary or intelligible relation between cause and effect that Berkeley denies causal power to matter and ideas. His understand-ing of cause and effect is very close to that of the French philosopher Nicolas Malebranche (1638-1715), who writes that "a true cause as I understand it is one such that the mind perceives a necessary connection between it and its effect" (*The Search after Truth*, Book 6, Part 2, chapter 3). Locke for example is willing to say that an event is a cause even if we are ignorant of its manner of operation (see *Essay* II xxvi 2). But Malebranche argues that if the manner of operation is unknown–if we do not understand why the second event *had to follow* from the first–

---

7. On the issues of this paragraph see Allaire, "Berkeley's Idealism."

then the attribution of causality is unjustified. Berkeley agrees with Malebranche. We will see in a moment how this agreement contributes to his conclusion that minds or spirits are the only true causes, a conclusion already suggested by the elimination of matter and perceived qualities as causal agents.

Berkeley believes that we ourselves are the spirits responsible for some of our ideas. "I find I can excite ideas in my mind at pleasure, and vary and shift the scene as oft as I think fit" (*Principles* 28). But ideas of sense are independent of our will:

> When in broad daylight I open my eyes, it is not in my power to choose whether I shall see or no, or to determine what particular objects shall present themselves to my view; and so likewise as to the hearing and other senses, the ideas imprinted on them are not creatures of my will. There is therefore some other will or spirit that produces them. (*Principles* 29)

That other will or spirit is God, and the patterns he imposes on ideas of sense are the laws of nature. Ideas, we learned above, are marks or signs; now experience becomes a text, with God its author and the laws of nature its grammar. God speaks to us through experience to promote our well-being; he informs us "that food nourishes, sleep refreshes, and fire warms us; that to sow in the seed-time is the way to reap in the harvest, and, in general, that to obtain such or such ends, such or such means are conducive" (*Principles* 31).

Berkeley follows Aristotle (384–322 B.C.) in distinguishing two kinds of cause: the efficient cause or agent, "that from which," according to Aristotle, "the change or the resting from change first begins," as the parent is the cause of the child, or the author of the book; and the final cause or end, "that for the sake of which a thing is," as health is the cause of a daily walk (Aristotle, *Metaphysics*, Book V, chapter 2). Berkeley thinks minds or spirits are involved in each kind of causation: minds are the only efficient causes, as well as the only things capable of acting for the sake of final causes or ends. Many of Berkeley's contemporaries agree with him on the latter point, but Berkeley differs from most of them in two connected ways. First, he believes that physicists, because they confine their investigations to the physical world, are not inquiring into genuine efficient causes. Physicists are the grammarians of the language of nature; they discover regularities (many of them useful), but explain nothing. Now if Berkeley is right about efficient causation, this deficiency in physics is very easy to correct. All the physicist has to do is point to God whenever anyone asks him for the cause of an event in nature. Can Berkeley honestly say this *explains* the event, without abandoning his high standard of explanation? This is where the second important difference between Berkeley and his contemporaries comes into play. Berkeley believes that we should seek to explain natural events by final causes, something René Descartes (1596-1650) and Baruch Spinoza (1632-1677), for example, both deny. "I see no reason," Berkeley writes, "why pointing out the various ends, to which natural things are adapted, and for which they were originally and with unspeakable wisdom contrived, should not be thought one good way of accounting for them, and altogether worthy a philosopher" (*Principles* 107). Berkeley thinks that if we do not simply identify God as the efficient cause of natural events, but supplement our identification with an account of the divine ends that the laws of nature serve, we will satisfy even the highest standard of explanation, because the connection between an arrangement and the intention behind it is not, he believes, a brute one. Intentions, on Berkeley's view, make arrangements intelligible: when we learn, for example, what an artist or builder was trying to achieve, we understand why his creation had to be the way it is. Thus Berkeley's high standard of explanation, which demands an intelligible connection between cause and effect, leads to the conclusion that minds are the only true efficient causes, because minds are the only things capable of intelligible action for the sake of an end.

(c) *Physical objects have two kinds of qualities,* primary *and* secondary. Locke's list of primary qualities includes solidity, extension, figure, motion or rest, and number. (Berkeley gives the same list at *Principles* 9.) When insensible particles unite to form an object, their primary qualities and spatial arrangement give the object what the scientist and philosopher Robert Boyle (1627-1691) calls its *texture.*[8] The texture is responsible for the object's power to produce ideas of secondary qualities in perceiving minds. Secondary qualities, Locke explains, are "nothing in the Objects themselves, but Powers to produce various Sensations in us by their *primary Qualities*" (*Essay* II viii 10).

When Berkeley outlines the distinction between primary and secondary qualities in sections 9 and 10, he writes as if its defenders believe that secondary qualities exist only in the mind. He argues, for example,

---

8. For Boyle's own discussion of qualities, which was an important influence on Locke's, see "The Origin of Forms and Qualities," especially pp. 18-41.

that because the two kinds of qualities cannot be conceived apart, primary qualities must exist where everyone agrees the secondary qualities exist–"to wit, in the mind and nowhere else" (*Principles* 10). This interpretation of the distinction is understandable: claims such as "*Light, Heat, Whiteness, or Coldness, are no more really in [things], than Sickness or Pain*" (*Essay* II viii 17) can easily suggest that the secondary qualities, like pain, exist only in the mind. But Locke is usually careful to distinguish between the secondary qualities themselves, which he takes to be powers in the object, and their effects, which are ideas in the mind. The point of the comparison with pain is not that the secondary qualities exist in the mind, but that they are (like painfulness) dispositions or powers. And as dispositions or powers, they depend on the object's texture–a texture that is in the object, whether or not it is perceived. This is what bothers Berkeley. "We have already shown," he writes in section 9, "that extension, figure and motion are only ideas existing in the mind." The distinction between primary and secondary qualities is just one more version of the belief in material substance, and Berkeley thinks his earlier arguments apply to it as a special case.[9]

(d) *It is impossible to* prove *that the physical world exists.* It may seem that Berkeley gives in to the skeptic, partly because he reduces things to ideas, and partly because his arguments are so often reminiscent of the skeptic's own. But Berkeley sounds like a skeptic only when it is the materialist's world that is up for discussion. He argues in sections 18 through 20, for example, that the existence of "substances without the mind" cannot be discovered by either sense or reason. It cannot be discovered by sense, because all we immediately perceive are our own ideas, beyond which the senses, being incapable of inference, cannot take us. It cannot be discovered by reason or inference, because there is no necessary or intelligible connection between ideas and matter. While Berkeley thinks skepticism is inevitable if we think of physical objects

9. In section 14, Berkeley observes that arguments from perceptual relativity work as well for primary qualities as they do for secondary qualities, a point he may have borrowed from Pierre Bayle (1647-1706) (see Popkin, "Berkeley and Pyrrhonism," and Bayle, *Historical and Critical Dictionary: Selections,* pp. 364-66). An argument from perceptual relativity maintains that a quality cannot exist in things themselves if its appearance varies with the position or state of the perceiver. It was once thought that Locke makes use of such arguments, but it has recently been shown that he does not. (See for example Curley, "Locke, Boyle, and the Distinction between Primary and Secondary Qualities.") For a defense of Berkeley as an interpreter of Locke's views on qualities see Stroud, "Berkeley *v.* Locke on Primary Qualities."

as materialists do, he thinks it becomes impossible once we conceive of them as he recommends.

According to Berkeley, expressions such as "body," "corporeal substance," and "external thing" have both philosophical and ordinary ("vulgar") senses. (See *Principles* 37 and 82.) Philosophers view a body or external thing as a substance independent of the mind, and must therefore acknowledge a gap between ideas and things. This gap is all the skeptic needs to argue that the existence of things can never be known. Since Berkeley contends that the philosophical notion of a thing is contradictory or empty, he cannot of course oppose the skeptic in the usual way, by asserting the existence of an external world in the philosophical sense. This causes him no regrets, however, because to speak of the world in the philosophical sense, he thinks, is to acknowledge the very gap between ideas and things that assures the skeptic's victory. The philosopher may ridicule the skeptic, or cultivate a casualness about the skeptic's conclusion (Locke's strategies in the *Essay*), but the only way to *defeat* the skeptic, Berkeley thinks, is to close the gap between ideas and things. If a veil of ideas intervenes between the mind and the world, the existence of things can never be known. But if things *are* ideas, our minds touch the world directly, and the skeptic's argument cannot even begin. We are left with a world of things in the ordinary sense, a world of things we touch, see, feel, and hear directly.

Berkeley cannot say that *all* ideas are things, or he will have no way of distinguishing between illusion and reality. Only ideas of sense – "the ideas imprinted on the senses by the Author of Nature" – are real (*Principles* 33). They count as real not because they correspond to external things (in the philosophical sense of "external"), but because they are more "regular, vivid, and constant," and "more strong, orderly, and coherent" than other ideas (*Principles* 33).

Berkeley's immaterialism faces a large number of objections. (Berkeley himself deals with fourteen different ones in sections 34 through 84.) I would like to discuss two that are especially important.

(1) *"Let's get back to the falling tree. It seems that Berkeley must say that with none of us around, the tree cannot even exist. It seems in general that the things in Berkeley's world lead an intermittent life, popping in and out of existence as our attention comes and goes, but this is absurd."*[10]

---

10. For an entertaining portrayal of students criticizing Berkeley's position along these lines, see the opening pages of E. M. Forster's novel, *The Longest Journey.*

Berkeley's reply is that "we may not conclude [objects] have no existence except only while they are perceived by *us*, since there may be some other spirit that perceives them, though we do not" (*Principles* 48, my italics). The reference to "some other spirit" is apparently a reference to God, a reading supported by *Three Dialogues* 2, where Philonous says that God perceives all things (*Works* II, p. 212; Adams, p. 47). But in the third dialogue, Philonous seems to retract his claim: "God, whom no external being can affect," he cautions, "perceives nothing by sense as we do" (p. 241; p. 74). The cause of Berkeley's wavering is an ambiguity in the word "perceive": in one sense it refers to the reception of uninvited ideas from an outside source (this is "perception by sense"); in another it refers to the simple existence of ideas in the mind, however they arrive there. God cannot perceive in the first sense because nothing can happen against his will, but there is no reason he cannot perceive in the second, as Philonous admits when he follows up his retraction with the assurance that "God knows or has ideas" (p. 241; p. 74). Does this mean that according to Berkeley, God is conserving every object we fail to notice by an act of universal perception? Although Berkeley often writes as if the answer is yes, he has, in fact, no need to do so. Recall that ideas are inert or passive by their very nature. They have no causal power, even if the mind perceiving them is God's. This is why Berkeley's account of ideas of sense appeals not to divine ideas but to divine acts of will: even if there were divine ideas, they would be, at best, superfluous accompaniments of divine action. An idea of sense cannot be made more real because there is a similar idea in the mind producing it. To borrow Berkeley's verdict on a similar hypothesis, though "we should allow it possible" that there is a divine idea for everything, it "must yet be a very unaccountable and extravagant supposition" (*Principles* 53). It might be replied that although divine ideas have no causal role to play, and therefore no contribution to make to the reality of ideas of sense, they are necessary to supply physical objects with their identities. Berkeley argues, after all, that physical objects are ideas, but he cannot identify them with human ideas, since he grants that objects may survive when no human mind perceives them. It seems that without divine ideas, there is nothing *with which to identify objects*. The tendency to think that there must be ideas with which objects can be identified is, admittedly, encouraged by Berkeley himself, as well as by my own exposition; but there is another tendency in Berkeley–a tendency which may be more profound–towards dispensing with the object altogether. We know that Berkeley's universe is occupied by a community of spirits, one of them infinite, the rest finite. The finite minds are filled with ideas, and the infinite spirit has a schedule for producing the most vivid and coherent sequences of those ideas, a schedule he can revise at any time. We are tempted to ask, "Where are the objects?," but in several places Berkeley suggests that this may be a bad question. At *Principles* 3, for example, he writes that "the table I write on, I say, exists, that is, I see and feel it; and if I were out of my study I should say it existed, meaning thereby that if I was in my study I might perceive it, or that some other spirit actually does perceive it." And when we say the earth moves, he explains at *Principles* 58, we mean that if we were favorably placed, "we should perceive the [earth] to move among the choir of the planets, and appearing in all respects like one of them." These two passages suggest that statements about physical objects are equivalent in meaning to statements about actual and possible perceptions. On such a view, to say that a tree falls in the forest when there is no one around to hear it is to say that if we enter the forest we will perceive a tree on the ground, and if we had been there earlier, we would have heard a sound. So understood, the statement demands no more for its truth than the existence of finite minds with ideas of sense, and an infinite mind with a schedule for their production. There need not be a particular cluster of ideas with which the tree can be identified. The tree remains mind-dependent, not because it is a cluster of ideas, but because it makes no sense to speak of the tree apart from human ideas and divine intentions to produce them. The view that statements about physical objects are equivalent in meaning to statements about perception is known as *phenomenalism.* It is often referred to as "Berkeley without God" by those who mistakenly suppose that the only role for God in Berkeley's universe is as the perceiver of unnoticed objects. But God's role in Berkeley's phenomenalist universe is an exalted one, since there can be no perceptions, actual or possible, unless there is a being capable of causing them. I do not think Berkeley finally decides which of the two roles God plays. The tendency to identify objects with ideas coexists with Berkeley's phenomenalism, and some of his most important arguments might not survive its elimination. There is, moreover, something undeniably comforting about the image of a perceiving God as the caretaker of a neglected world, supporting it all with his infinite attention and concern. But in a phenomenalist universe God's concern lies more directly with *us,* a fact that impresses Berkeley deeply. But we must now turn to the second objection.

(2) *"How can Berkeley be so sure that minds or spirits actually exist? He will have a hard time explaining how we manage even to think of them. He*

argues in section 27, and again in sections 135 through 139, that we cannot have an idea of spirit, because ideas represent only what they resemble, and passive ideas and active spirits are in no way alike. But if we cannot have ideas of spirits, we can neither think of them nor know them."

Berkeley never gives an account of our ability to think of spirits, and he seems to think he doesn't have to. There is a widespread impression that he attempts such an account, an impression created by his use of the word "notion." In the first edition of the *Principles*, Berkeley uses the word "notion" as a synonym for "idea." But in the second, though there is no change of doctrine, "notion" acquires a technical sense: it becomes whatever we "have" when we think of minds or spirits, or understand the words that signify them. "We have some notion of soul, spirit, and the operations of the mind," he adds to section 27 in the second edition, "inasmuch as we know or understand the meaning of those words." (The same point is made in both editions, but in the first edition without the word "notion," at section 140.) But it is a mistake to suppose that notions stand to spirits as ideas stand to things. A notion, for Berkeley, is not a representing entity. When he says we have a notion of spirit, he is not trying to account for our ability to think and speak of spirits by identifying an object of thought that stands for them; he is simply saying, in a long-winded way, that we do have the ability. He has been attacked for this, because it looks as if he is more lenient with spiritual substance than he is with matter. He anticipates this criticism in both the *Principles* and the *Three Dialogues*. His main response in the *Principles* is that our ability to think of spirits—an ability displayed by each of us when he thinks of his own self—is too obvious to need explaining. "What I am myself, that which I denote by the term I, is the same with what is meant by *soul* or *spiritual substance*." (*Principles* 139. For the response in the *Dialogues*, which is in some ways more satisfying, see *Works* II, pp. 232-33; Adams, pp. 66-67.)

With our ability to think of spirits established, Berkeley proceeds to discuss our knowledge of them. He says "we comprehend our own existence by inward feeling or reflection, and that of other spirits by reason" (*Principles* 89). We infer the existence of other finite spirits from the "several motions, changes, and combinations of ideas, that inform [us] there are certain particular agents like [ourselves], which accompany them, and concur in their production" (*Principles* 145). The existence of God is inferred from the existence of ideas of sense, and from their regularity, harmony, and perfection (see *Principles* 146). Because the body of ideas caused by God is so much greater than the body of ideas associated with any finite spirit, "the existence of God is far more evidently perceived than the existence of men" (*Principles* 147).

We now see why Berkeley cannot accept the view that every significant word stands for an idea: words that refer to spirits cannot stand for ideas. Berkeley not only denies the content assumption, but is prepared in some cases to do without a mental object altogether.[11]

3. *The structure and intent of the* Principles

Why does Berkeley begin the *Principles* by attacking abstract ideas? At *Principles* 5 he writes that materialism "will, perhaps, be found at bottom to depend on the doctrine of *abstract ideas*. For can there be a nicer strain of abstraction than to distinguish the existence of sensible objects from their being perceived?" This suggests that the attack on abstraction is supposed to provide an argument against materialism, but on the interpretation of the Introduction I offer in section 1, it is doubtful such an argument is possible. In order to know that the idea of an unperceived object is abstract, we must already know that there can be no unperceived objects, but if we know that, materialism has already been disposed of. That the materialist is guilty of abstraction is something Berkeley might derive as a conclusion, but not something he can claim as a premise. But then what does the Introduction have to do with Part I?

Although the Introduction is devoted mainly to abstract ideas, Berkeley says that it concerns "the nature and abuse of language" (Introduction 6), and the closing sections make it clear that the point of the Introduction is to change our attitude towards words. After completing his attack on abstraction, Berkeley traces the doctrine to language – specifically, to the assumption that every significant name stands for a particular idea (Introduction 20). This assumption is stated more fully at *Principles* 116, where Berkeley writes that "we are apt to think every noun substantive stands for a distinct idea, that may be separated from all others." Berkeley thinks this assumption has disastrous consequences when applied to two noun substantives in particular: the words "existence" and "perception." For if each of these words stands for an idea "that may be separated from all others" – including the idea associated with the other word in the pair – then existence and perception can be conceived apart. But anything conceivable is possi-

---

11. Berkeley's denial that every word stands for an idea is deepened and extended in *Alciphron* VII. See also Introduction to the *Principles* 19–20.

ble. It therefore follows that there can be existence without perception. And this, of course, is materialism. The problem, as Berkeley sees it, is that relations among words are an unreliable guide to relations among things. If we want to know whether there can be existence without perception, it is a mistake to ask whether the words "existence" and "perception" can occur apart, or whether the definition of the first includes the second. The aim of the Introduction is to diminish our confidence in such linguistic tests of possibility.[12] When Berkeley urges us to "draw the curtain of words" (Introduction 24), he is not recommending a vague stare at our ideas and mental operations, but a concentration on their separability and inseparability, in the hope that when he tells us in Part I that existence and perception are inseparable, we will look past words and agree. The importance he attaches to this concentration is brought out at *Principles* 22, where he offers to rest his whole case on a single point. If anyone can *conceive* of an object outside the mind, Berkeley writes, he will grant that it exists:

> But say you, surely there is nothing easier than to imagine trees, for instance, in a park, or books existing in a closet, and nobody by to perceive them. I answer, you may so, there is no difficulty in it: but what is all this, I beseech you, more than framing in your mind certain ideas which you call *books* and *trees*, and at the same time omitting to frame the idea of anyone that may perceive them? But do not you yourself perceive or think of them all the while? (*Principles* 23. See also section 6.)

I would like to close this introduction with two remarks about Berkeley's philosophical style and aim. The first is that Berkeley is a dialectician: the medium of his philosophy is argument or debate. In his notebooks, for example, he defines his position against the views of Locke and Malebranche. In spite of his warnings against being imposed on by words, he arrives at his philosophy not by looking at the world (or even at his ideas), but by reading books. He thrives on replying to objections—in the *Principles* he spends twice as much time in a give-and-take with imaginary critics as he spends on his positive argument—and this is one reason he finds the dialogue-form of the *Three Dialogues* and *Alciphron* so congenial. His aim is always to convince his opponent, and he regularly makes use of his opponent's premises in his

---

12. The objective test of possibility I discuss on pp. xvii–xviii can be construed as a linguistic test. This is one more expression of the tension between Berkeley's demand for an objective test and the conclusions he hopes to establish.

own arguments. What all this means is that any reader who hopes to criticize Berkeley should pay particular attention to the assumptions Berkeley shares (or thinks he shares) with the philosophers he opposes, for example, the assumption that we immediately perceive only our own ideas.

The second point is that Berkeley does not think of himself as a scholarly professional advancing an academic specialty. His aim is not to make a contribution to an enduring field of study, but to turn us away from the useless speculation generated by past mistakes, so we can devote more time to God, our duty, and the ordinary business of life. He makes these points in the closing sections of the *Principles*, but brings them out even more effectively, by literary means, at the beginning of the *Three Dialogues*. Philonous is surprised to find Hylas up so early. Hylas admits it is "something unusual," but explains that he was so excited by a philosophical conversation of the night before that he was unable to get to sleep. This tells us why Hylas gets up late every morning: he is always up late talking about philosophy. Philonous then makes a long speech celebrating the early-morning pleasures Hylas usually misses ("that purple sky, these wild but sweet notes of birds, the fragrant bloom upon the trees and flowers"), and a moment later he begins to make his case for immaterialism. "Listen to me," Berkeley is saying, "and you can stop doing philosophy, and get on to more important things." Like some other great philosophers, Berkeley thought philosophy would somehow end with him; like them, what made him great is not that he ended it, but that he made it even harder to avoid.[13]

13. I am grateful to Robert M. Adams, Jonathan Adler, Owen Flanagan, Allan Janik, and Linda Gardiner for their comments on earlier versions of this essay.

Chronology of Berkeley's Life

1734   Consecrated Bishop of Cloyne. He serves his diocese for
       nearly twenty years.
       *The Analyst, or A Discourse Addressed to an Infidel Mathe-
       matician*

1735   *A Defence of Free-thinking in Mathematics*

1744   *Siris: a Chain of Philosophical Reflections and Inquiries
       concerning the Virtues of Tar-water, and divers other sub-
       jects*

1753   Dies at Oxford

Selected Bibliography

WORKS BY BERKELEY

Robert Merrihew Adams (ed.), *Three Dialogues between Hylas and Philonous*. Indianapolis: Hackett Publishing Company, 1979.

A. A. Luce and T. E. Jessop (eds.), *The Works of George Berkeley, Bishop of Cloyne;* 9 volumes. London: Nelson, 1948–57.

BIOGRAPHIES

Edwin S. Gaustad, *George Berkeley in America*. New Haven: Yale University Press, 1979.

A. A. Luce, *The Life of George Berkeley, Bishop of Cloyne*. London: Nelson, 1949.

BIBLIOGRAPHIES

T. E. Jessop, *A Bibliography of George Berkeley*. London: Oxford University Press, 1934; second edition revised and enlarged, The Hague: Nijhoff, 1973.

C. M. Turbayne and Robert Ware, "A Bibliography of George Berkeley, 1933–1962," *Journal of Philosophy* 60 (1963), pp. 93–112.

For 1963–79 see pp. 313–29 in Turbayne (ed.), *Berkeley: Critical and Interpretive Essays* (listed below under "ANTHOLOGIES"); for 1980–85 see pp. 243–60 in Sosa (ed.), *Essays on the Philosophy of George Berkeley* (also listed below). Recent items on Berkeley are listed in the *Berkeley Newsletter*, published yearly at Trinity College, Dublin.

ANTHOLOGIES ON BERKELEY

David Berman (ed.), *George Berkeley: Essays and Replies*. Dublin: Irish Academic Press, 1986.

John Foster and Howard Robinson (eds.), *Essays on Berkeley: A Tercentennial Celebration*. Oxford: Clarendon Press, 1985.

C. B. Martin and David Armstrong (eds.), *Locke and Berkeley*. Garden City, New York: Doubleday, 1968; Notre Dame: University of Notre Dame Press, 1968.

S. C. Pepper, Karl Aschenbrenner, and Benson Mates (eds.), *George Berkeley*, University of California Publications in Philosophy, volume 29. Berkeley and Los Angeles: University of California Press, 1957.

Ernest Sosa (ed.), *Essays on the Philosophy of George Berkeley*. Dordrecht: D. Reidel, 1987.

Colin Murray Turbayne (ed.), *Berkeley: Critical and Interpretive Essays*. Minneapolis: University of Minnesota Press, 1982.

BOOKS AND ARTICLES ON BERKELEY

Robert M. Adams, "Berkeley's 'Notion' of Spiritual Substance," *Archiv für Geschichte der Philosophie* 55 (1973), pp. 47–69.

Edwin B. Allaire, "Berkeley's Idealism," *Theoria* 29 (1963), pp. 229–44.

Margaret Atherton, *Berkeley's Revolution in Vision*. Ithaca: Cornell University Press, 1990.

M. R. Ayers, "Substance, Reality, and the Great, Dead Philosophers," *American Philosophical Quarterly* 7 (1970), pp. 38–49.

Jonathan Bennett, *Locke, Berkeley, Hume: Central Themes*. Oxford: Oxford University Press, 1971.

David Berman, *George Berkeley: Idealism and the Man*. Oxford: Clarendon Press, 1994.

Harry Bracken, *Berkeley*. London: Macmillan, 1974.

——, *The Early Reception of Berkeley's Immaterialism, 1710–1733*, revised edition. The Hague: Nijhoff, 1965.

Richard J. Brook, *Berkeley's Philosophy of Science*. The Hague: Nijhoff, 1973.

E. J. Craig, "Berkeley's Attack on Abstract Ideas," *Philosophical Review* 77 (1968), pp. 425–37.

Jonathan Dancy, *Berkeley: An Introduction*. Oxford: Blackwell, 1987.

A. C. Grayling, *Berkeley: The Central Arguments*. La Salle, Illinois: Open Court, 1986.

A. A. Luce, *Berkeley and Malebranche*. Oxford: Oxford University Press, 1934.

——, *Berkeley's Immaterialism*. London: Nelson, 1945.

——, *The Dialectic of Immaterialism*. London: Hodder and Stoughton, 1963.

Robert Muehlmann, *Berkeley's Ontology*. Indianapolis: Hackett Publishing Company, 1992.

George Pitcher, *Berkeley*. London: Routledge & Kegan Paul, 1977.

Richard H. Popkin, "Berkeley and Pyrrhonism," *Review of Metaphysics* 5 (1951–2), pp. 223–46.

Barry Stroud, "Berkeley *v.* Locke on Primary Qualities," *Philosophy* 55 (1980), pp. 149–66.

C. C. W. Taylor, "Berkeley's Theory of Abstract Ideas," *Philosophical Quarterly* 28 (1978), pp. 97–115.

Ian C. Tipton, *Berkeley: The Philosophy of Immaterialism*. London: Methuen, 1974.

J. O. Urmson, *Berkeley*. Oxford: Oxford University Press, 1982.

Julius Weinberg, "The Nominalism of Berkeley and Hume." In *Abstraction, Relation, and Induction: Three Essays in the History of Thought*, by Julius Weinberg, pp. 3–60. Madison: University of Wisconsin Press, 1965.

Kenneth P. Winkler, *Berkeley: An Interpretation*. Oxford: Clarendon Press, 1989.

OTHER WORKS CITED IN THE EDITOR'S INTRODUCTION OR THE NOTES

Aristotle, *Metaphysics*. In *The Complete Works of Aristotle*, edited by Jonathan Barnes, volume 1. Princeton: Princeton University Press, 1984.

Pierre Bayle, *Historical and Critical Dictionary: Selections*, translated with an introduction and notes by Richard Popkin. Indianapolis: Bobbs-Merrill, 1965. Reprinted 1991 by Hackett Publishing Company, Inc.

Robert Boyle, "The Origin of Forms and Qualities According to the Corpuscular Philosophy." In *Selected Philosophical Papers of Robert Boyle*, edited by M. A. Stewart, pp. 1–96. Manchester: Manchester University Press, 1979.

E. M. Curley, "Locke, Boyle, and the Distinction between Primary and Secondary Qualities," *Philosophical Review* 81 (1972), pp. 438–64.

René Descartes, The Principles of Philosophy, Part I. In *The Philosophical Writings of Descartes*, volume 1, translated by John Cottinghan,

Robert Stoothuff, and Dugald Murdoch. Cambridge: Cambridge University Press, 1984.

John Locke, *An Essay concerning Human Understanding,* edited by P. H. Nidditch. Oxford: Oxford University Press, 1975.

J. L. Mackie, *Problems from Locke.* Oxford: Oxford University Press, 1976.

Nicolas Malebranche, *The Search after Truth,* translated by Thomas M. Lennon and Paul J. Olscamp. Columbus: Ohio State University Press, 1980.

Isaac Newton, *Mathematical Principles of Natural Philosophy,* a revision of Andrew Motte's translation by Florian Cajori. Berkeley: University of California Press, 1934.

John Norris, *An Essay towards the Theory of the Ideal or Intelligible World,* 2 volumes. London: Printed for S. Manship; and W. Hawes, 1701-4.

John Redwood, *Reason, Ridicule and Religion: The Age of Enlightenment in England, 1600-1750.* Cambridge: Harvard University Press, 1976.

Baruch Spinoza, *The Ethics,* translated by Samuel Shirley, edited by Seymour Feldman. Indianapolis: Hackett Publishing Company, Inc., 1992.

A Note on the Text

The text is based on the second edition (London, 1734), the last one published in Berkeley's lifetime. I have included the letter of dedication and the Preface from the first edition, published in Dublin in 1710. Passages new to the second edition are identified by brackets and footnotes, and some other important differences between the two editions are explained in the notes.

About the text as it appears:

1. I have changed Berkeley's spelling to conform to contemporary American custom. The most drastic changes: collapsing "it self" and similar expressions into single words, and substituting "does" and "has" for "doth" and "hath."

2. Berkeley capitalizes most nouns, some verbs and adjectives, and usually the first word following a colon. All this has been modernized. Where Berkeley puts whole words in capitals for emphasis, I have left the first letter capitalized.

3. Berkeley uses semicolons and colons where we would use commas or periods (and sometimes uses periods where we would insist on commas or semicolons), but I have decided to leave his punctuation as it is. Yeats said that Berkeley remains "no matter what the theme, a conversationalist," and if the reader takes the frequent colons and semicolons as conversational stops and starts, he will find that they actually make the text easier to read. In one case, where it clarifies the sense, I have followed the punctuation of the first edition.

4. I have retained all of Berkeley's italics.

5. In the second edition Berkeley numbers his sections with Roman numerals. I have used Arabic numerals, as Berkeley does in the first edition.

6. Berkeley's only footnote is indicated by an asterisk; my own are numbered. Passages from the first edition are printed in italics when included in the notes. I refer to Berkeley's works by an abbreviated title, followed by a dialogue, section, or entry number. In the case of the *Three Dialogues* I also give volume and page number in the Luce and Jessop edition of the *Works*, and page number in Adams' edition of the *Dialogues*. Details on works cited can be found in the chronology and bibliography.

I am grateful to the Houghton Library of Harvard University for permitting me to make a copy of the 1734 edition, and to the Clapp

Library of Wellesley College for use of its copy of the 1710 edition. I am also grateful to Eleanor Nicholes, special collections librarian at the Clapp, for her advice and help, and to Janie Penn for proofreading the text.

For the 1995 printing I have updated the bibliography and made a number of small corrections elsewhere in the volume.

Wellesley, Massachusetts   KENNETH P. WINKLER

A TREATISE CONCERNING THE
PRINCIPLES OF HUMAN KNOWLEDGE

TO THE

Right Honorable

THOMAS

EARL OF

PEMBROKE, ETC.

Knight of the *Most Noble Order*

of the GARTER,

AND

One of the *Lords* of her

MAJESTY'S Most Honorable

PRIVY COUNCIL.[1]

MY LORD,

You'll, perhaps, wonder that an obscure person, who has not the honor to be known to your lordship, should presume to address you in this manner. But that a man, who has written something with a design to promote *useful knowledge* and *religion* in the world, should make choice of your lordship for his patron, will not be thought strange by anyone that is not altogether unacquainted with the present state of the Church and learning, and consequently ignorant how great an ornament and support you are to both. Yet, nothing could have induced me to make you this present of my poor endeavors, were I not encouraged by that candor and native goodness, which is so bright a part in your lordship's character. I might add, my lord, that the extraordinary favor and bounty you have been pleased to show towards our Society, gave me hopes, you'd not be unwilling to countenance the studies of one of its members.[2] These considerations determined me to lay this treatise at your lordship's feet. And the rather, because I was ambitious to have it

1. The letter of dedication was omitted in the second edition.
2. "our Society" is Trinity College, Dublin, where Berkeley was a fellow and tutor.

known, that I am with the truest and most profound respect, on account of that learning and virtue which the world so justly admires in your lordship,

> *My Lord,*
>> *Your Lordship's*
>>> *Most Humble*
>>>> *And Most Devoted*
>>>>> *Servant.*
>>>>>> George Berkeley.

THE PREFACE.[1]

WHAT *I here make public has, after a long and scrupulous inquiry, seemed to me evidently true, and not unuseful to be known, particularly to those who are tainted with skepticism, or want a demonstration of the existence and immateriality of God, or the natural immortality of the soul. Whether it be so or no, I am content the reader should impartially examine. Since I do not think myself any farther concerned for the success of what I have written, than as it is agreeable to* truth. *But to the end* this *may not suffer, I make it my request that the reader suspend his judgment, till he has once,* at least, *read the whole through with that degree of attention and thought which the subject matter shall seem to deserve. For as there are some passages that, taken by themselves, are very liable (nor could it be remedied) to gross misinterpretation, and to be charged with most absurd consequences, which, nevertheless, upon an entire perusal will appear not to follow from them: so likewise, though the whole should be read over, yet, if this be done transiently, 'tis very probable my sense may be mistaken; but to a thinking reader, I flatter myself, it will be throughout clear and obvious. As for the characters of novelty and singularity, which some of the following notions may seem to bear, 'tis, I hope, needless to make any apology on that account. He must surely be either very weak, or very little acquainted with the sciences, who shall reject a truth, that is capable of demonstration, for no other reason but because it's newly known and contrary to the prejudices of mankind. Thus much I thought fit to premise, in order to prevent, if possible, the hasty censures of a sort of men, who are too apt to condemn an opinion before they rightly comprehend it.*

---

1. The Preface was omitted in the second edition.

INTRODUCTION.

1. Philosophy being nothing else but the study of wisdom and truth, it may with reason be expected, that those who have spent most time and pains in it should enjoy a greater calm and serenity of mind, a greater clearness and evidence of knowledge, and be less disturbed with doubts and difficulties than other men. Yet so it is we see the illiterate bulk of mankind that walk the high-road of plain, common sense, and are governed by the dictates of nature, for the most part easy and undisturbed. To them nothing that's familiar appears unaccountable or difficult to comprehend. They complain not of any want of evidence in their senses, and are out of all danger of becoming *skeptics*. But no sooner do we depart from sense and instinct to follow the light of a superior principle, to reason, meditate, and reflect on the nature of things, but a thousand scruples spring up in our minds, concerning those things which before we seemed fully to comprehend. Prejudices and errors of sense do from all parts discover themselves to our view; and endeavoring to correct these by reason we are insensibly drawn into uncouth paradoxes, difficulties, and inconsistencies, which multiply and grow upon us as we advance in speculation; till at length, having wandered through many intricate mazes, we find ourselves just where we were, or, which is worse, sit down in a forlorn skepticism.

2. The cause of this is thought to be the obscurity of things, or the natural weakness and imperfection of our understandings. It is said the faculties we have are few, and those designed by nature for the support and comfort of life, and not to penetrate into the inward essence and constitution of things. Besides, the mind of man being finite, when it treats of things which partake of infinity, it is not to be wondered at, if it run into absurdities and contradictions; out of which it is impossible it should ever extricate itself, it being of the nature of infinite not to be comprehended by that which is finite.

3. But perhaps we may be too partial to ourselves in placing the fault originally in our faculties, and not rather in the wrong use we make of them. It is a hard thing to suppose, that right deductions from true principles should ever end in consequences which cannot be maintained or made consistent. We should believe that God has dealt more bountifully with the sons of men, than to give them a strong desire for that knowledge, which he had placed quite out of their reach. This were not

agreeable to the wonted, indulgent methods of providence, which, whatever appetites it may have implanted in the creatures, does usually furnish them with such means as, if rightly made use of, will not fail to satisfy them. Upon the whole, I am inclined to think that the far greater part, if not all, of those difficulties which have hitherto amused philosophers, and blocked up the way to knowledge, are entirely owing to ourselves. That we have first raised a dust, and then complain, we cannot see.

4. My purpose therefore is, to try if I can discover what those principles are, which have introduced all that doubtfulness and uncertainty, those absurdities and contradictions into the several sects of philosophy; insomuch that the wisest men have thought our ignorance incurable, conceiving it to arise from the natural dullness and limitation of our faculties. And surely it is a work well deserving our pains, to make a strict inquiry concerning the first principles of *human knowledge,* to sift and examine them on all sides: especially since there may be some grounds to suspect that those lets and difficulties, which stay and embarrass the mind in its search after truth, do not spring from any darkness and intricacy in the objects, or natural defect in the understanding, so much as from false principles which have been insisted on, and might have been avoided.

5. How difficult and discouraging soever this attempt may seem, when I consider how many great and extraordinary men have gone before me in the same designs: yet I am not without some hopes, upon the consideration that the largest views are not always the clearest, and that he who is short-sighted will be obliged to draw the object nearer, and may, perhaps, by a close and narrow survey discern that which had escaped far better eyes.

6. In order to prepare the mind of the reader for the easier conceiving what follows, it is proper to premise somewhat, by way of introduction, concerning the nature and abuse of language. But the unraveling this matter leads me in some measure to anticipate my design, by taking notice of what seems to have had a chief part in rendering speculation intricate and perplexed, and to have occasioned innumerable errors and difficulties in almost all parts of knowledge. And that is the opinion that the mind has a power of framing *abstract ideas* or notions of things. He who is not a perfect stranger to the writings and disputes of philosophers, must needs acknowledge that no small part of them are spent

about abstract ideas. These are in a more especial manner, thought to be the object of those sciences which go by the name of *logic* and *metaphysics,* and of all that which passes under the notion of the most abstracted and sublime learning, in all which one shall scarce find any question handled in such a manner, as does not suppose their existence in the mind, and that it is well acquainted with them.

7. It is agreed on all hands, that the qualities or modes of things do never really exist each of them apart by itself, and separated from all others, but are mixed, as it were, and blended together, several in the same object. But we are told, the mind being able to consider each quality singly, or abstracted from those other qualities with which it is united, does by that means frame to itself abstract ideas. For example, there is perceived by sight an object extended, colored, and moved: this mixed or compound idea the mind resolving into its simple, constituent parts, and viewing each by itself, exclusive of the rest, does frame the abstract ideas of extension, color, and motion. Not that it is possible for color or motion to exist without extension: but only that the mind can frame to itself by *abstraction* the idea of color exclusive of extension, and of motion exclusive of both color and extension.

8. Again, the mind having observed that in the particular extensions perceived by sense, there is something common and alike in all, and some other things peculiar, as this or that figure or magnitude, which distinguish them one from another; it considers apart or singles out by itself that which is common, making thereof a most abstract idea of extension, which is neither line, surface, nor solid, nor has any figure or magnitude but is an idea entirely prescinded from all these. So likewise the mind by leaving out of the particular colors perceived by sense, that which distinguishes them one from another, and retaining that only which is common to all, makes an idea of color in abstract which is neither red, nor blue, nor white, nor any other determinate color. And in like manner by considering motion abstractedly not only from the body moved, but likewise from the figure it describes, and all particular directions and velocities, the abstract idea of motion is framed; which equally corresponds to all particular motions whatsoever that may be perceived by sense.

9. And as the mind frames to itself abstract ideas of qualities or modes, so does it, by the same precision or mental separation, attain abstract ideas of the more compounded beings, which include several coexistent

qualities. For example, the mind having observed that *Peter, James,* and *John,* resemble each other, in certain common agreements of shape and other qualities, leaves out of the complex or compounded idea it has of *Peter, James,* and any other particular man, that which is peculiar to each, retaining only what is common to all; and so makes an abstract idea wherein all the particulars equally partake, abstracting entirely from and cutting off all those circumstances and differences, which might determine it to any particular existence. And after this manner it is said we come by the abstract idea of *man* or, if you please, humanity or human nature; wherein it is true there is included color, because there is no man but has some color, but then it can be neither white, nor black, nor any particular color; because there is no one particular color wherein all men partake. So likewise there is included stature, but then it is neither tall stature nor low stature, nor yet middle stature, but something abstracted from all these. And so of the rest. Moreover, there being a great variety of other creatures that partake in some parts, but not all, of the complex idea of *man,* the mind leaving out those parts which are peculiar to men, and retaining those only which are common to all the living creatures, frames the idea of *animal,* which abstracts not only from all particular men, but also all birds, beasts, fishes, and insects. The constituent parts of the abstract idea of animal are body, life, sense, and spontaneous motion. By *body* is meant, body without any particular shape or figure, there being no one shape or figure common to all animals, without covering, either of hair or feathers, or scales, etc. nor yet naked: hair, feathers, scales, and nakedness being the distinguishing properties of particular animals, and for that reason left out of the *abstract idea.* Upon the same account the spontaneous motion must be neither walking, nor flying, nor creeping, it is nevertheless a motion, but what that motion is, it is not easy to conceive.

10. Whether others have this wonderful faculty of *abstracting their ideas,* they best can tell: for myself I find indeed I have a faculty of imagining, or representing to myself the ideas of those particular things I have perceived and of variously compounding and dividing them. I can imagine a man with two heads or the upper parts of a man joined to the body of a horse. I can consider the hand, the eye, the nose, each by itself abstracted or separated from the rest of the body. But then whatever hand or eye I imagine, it must have some particular shape and color. Likewise the idea of man that I frame to myself, must be either of a white, or a black, or a tawny, a straight, or a crooked, a tall, or a low, or a

middle-sized man. I cannot by any effort of thought conceive the abstract idea above described. And it is equally impossible for me to form the abstract idea of motion distinct from the body moving, and which is neither swift nor slow, curvilinear nor rectilinear; and the like may be said of all other abstract general ideas whatsoever. To be plain, I own myself able to abstract in one sense, as when I consider some particular parts or qualities separated from others, with which though they are united in some object, yet, it is possible they may really exist without them. But I deny that I can abstract one from another, or conceive separately, those qualities which it is impossible should exist so separated; or that I can frame a general notion by abstracting from particulars in the manner aforesaid. Which two last are the proper acceptations of *abstraction*. And there are grounds to think most men will acknowledge themselves to be in my case. The generality of men which are simple and illiterate never pretend to *abstract notions*. It is said they are difficult and not to be attained without pains and study. We may therefore reasonably conclude that, if such there be, they are confined only to the learned.

11. I proceed to examine what can be alleged in defense of the doctrine of abstraction, and try if I can discover what it is that inclines the men of speculation to embrace an opinion, so remote from common sense as that seems to be. There has been a late deservedly esteemed philosopher, who, no doubt, has given it very much countenance by seeming to think the having abstract general ideas is what puts the widest difference in point of understanding betwixt man and beast.[1] "The having of general ideas (*says he*) is that which puts a perfect distinction betwixt man and brutes, and is an excellency which the faculties of brutes do by no means attain unto. For it is evident we observe no footsteps in them of making use of general signs for universal ideas; from which we have reason to imagine that they have not the faculty of *abstracting* or making general ideas, since they have no use of words or any other general signs. *And a little after.* Therefore, I think, we may suppose that it is in this that the species of brutes are discriminated from men, and 'tis that proper difference wherein they are wholly separated, and which at last widens to so wide a distance. For if they have any ideas at all, and are not bare machines (as some would have them) we cannot deny them to have some

---

1. The philosopher is John Locke (1632-1704), whose *An Essay concerning Human Understanding* was first published in 1690. Berkeley refers to passages in the *Essay* by book, chapter, and section. I follow the same practice in the footnotes.

reason. It seems as evident to me that they do some of them in certain instances reason as that they have sense, but it is only in particular ideas, just as they receive them from their senses. They are the best of them tied up within those narrow bounds, and have not (as I think) the faculty to enlarge them by any kind of *abstraction." Essay on Hum. Underst.* B. 2. C. 11. Sect. 10 and 11. I readily agree with this learned author, that the faculties of brutes can by no means attain to *abstraction.* But then if this be made the distinguishing property of that sort of animals, I fear a great many of those that pass for men must be reckoned into their number. The reason that is here assigned why we have no grounds to think brutes have abstract general ideas, is that we observe in them no use of words or any other general signs; which is built on this supposition, to wit, that the making use of words, implies the having general ideas. From which it follows, that men who use language are able to abstract or generalize their ideas. That this is the sense and arguing of the author will further appear by his answering the question he in another place puts. "Since all things that exist are only particulars, how come we by general terms? *His answer is,* Words become general by being made the signs of general ideas." *Essay on Hum. Underst.* B. 3. C. 3. *Sect.* 6. But it seems that a word becomes general by being made the sign, not of an abstract general idea but, of several particular ideas, any one of which it indifferently suggests to the mind. For example, when it is said *the change of motion is proportional to the impressed force,* or that *whatever has extension is divisible;* these propositions are to be understood of motion and extension in general, and nevertheless it will not follow that they suggest to my thoughts an idea of motion without a body moved, or any determinate direction and velocity, or that I must conceive an abstract general idea of extension, which is neither line, surface nor solid, neither great nor small, black, white, nor red, nor of any other determinate color. It is only implied that whatever motion I consider, whether it be swift or slow, perpendicular, horizontal or oblique, or in whatever object, the axiom concerning it holds equally true. As does the other of every particular extension, it matters not whether line, surface or solid, whether of this or that magnitude or figure.

12. By observing how ideas become general, we may the better judge how words are made so. And here it is to be noted that I do not deny absolutely there are general ideas, but only that there are any *abstract general ideas:* for in the passages above quoted, wherein there is mention

of general ideas, it is always supposed that they are formed by *abstraction*, after the manner set forth in *Sect.* 8 and 9. Now if we will annex a meaning to our words, and speak only of what we can conceive, I believe we shall acknowledge, that an idea, which considered in itself is particular, becomes general, by being made to represent or stand for all other particular ideas of the same sort. To make this plain by an example, suppose a geometrician is demonstrating the method, of cutting a line in two equal parts. He draws, for instance, a black line of an inch in length, this which in itself is a particular line is nevertheless with regard to its signification general, since as it is there used, it represents all particular lines whatsoever; so that what is demonstrated of it, is demonstrated of all lines, or, in other words, of a line in general. And as that particular line becomes general, by being made a sign, so the name *line* which taken absolutely is particular, by being a sign is made general. And as the former owes its generality, not to its being the sign of an abstract or general line, but of all particular right lines that may possibly exist, so the latter must be thought to derive its generality from the same cause, namely, the various particular lines which it indifferently denotes.

13. To give the reader a yet clearer view of the nature of abstract ideas, and the uses they are thought necessary to, I shall add one more passage out of the *Essay on Human Understanding*, which is as follows. "*Abstract ideas* are not so obvious or easy to children or the yet unexercised mind as particular ones. If they seem so to grown men, it is only because by constant and familiar use they are made so. For when we nicely reflect upon them, we shall find that general ideas are fictions and contrivances of the mind, that carry difficulty with them, and do not so easily offer themselves, as we are apt to imagine. For example, does it not require some pains and skill to form the general idea of a triangle (which is yet none of the most abstract comprehensive and difficult) for it must be neither oblique nor rectangle, neither equilateral, equicrural, nor scalenon, but *all and none* of these at once. In effect, it is something imperfect that cannot exist, an idea wherein some parts of several different and *inconsistent* ideas are put together. It is true the mind in this imperfect state has need of such ideas, and makes all the haste to them it can, for the conveniency of communication and enlargement of knowledge, to both which it is naturally very much inclined. But yet one has reason to suspect such ideas are marks of our imperfection. At least this is enough to show that the most abstract and general ideas are not those that the

mind is first and most easily acquainted with, nor such as its earliest knowledge is conversant about. B. 4. C. 7. Sect. 9."[2] If any man has the faculty of framing in his mind such an idea of a triangle as is here described, it is in vain to pretend to dispute him out of it, nor would I go about it. All I desire is, that the reader would fully and certainly inform himself whether he has such an idea or no. And this, methinks, can be no hard task for anyone to perform. What more easy than for anyone to look a little into his own thoughts, and there try whether he has, or can attain to have, an idea that shall correspond with the description that is here given of the general idea of a triangle, which is, *neither oblique, nor rectangle, equilateral, equicrural, nor scalenon, but all and none of these at once?*

14. Much is here said of the difficulty that abstract ideas carry with them, and the pains and skill requisite to the forming them. And it is on all hands agreed that there is need of great toil and labor of the mind, to emancipate our thoughts from particular objects, and raise them to those sublime speculations that are conversant about abstract ideas. From all which the natural consequence should seem to be, that so difficult a thing as the forming abstract ideas was not necessary for *communication,* which is so easy and familiar to all sorts of men. But we are told, if they seem obvious and easy to grown men, *it is only because by constant and familiar use they are made so.* Now I would fain know at what time it is, men are employed in surmounting that difficulty, and furnishing themselves with those necessary helps for discourse. It cannot be when they are grown up, for then it seems they are not conscious of any such pains-taking; it remains therefore to be the business of their childhood. And surely, the great and multiplied labor of framing abstract notions, will be found a hard task for that tender age. Is it not a hard thing to imagine, that a couple of children cannot prate together, of their sugar-plums and rattles and the rest of their little trinkets, till they have first tacked together numberless inconsistencies, and so framed in their minds *abstract general ideas,* and annexed them to every common name they make use of?

15. Nor do I think them a whit more needful for the *enlargement of knowledge* than for *communication.* It is I know a point much insisted on, that all knowledge and demonstration are about universal notions, to which I fully agree: but then it does not appear to me that those notions

---

2. The emphasis on "all and none" and "inconsistent" is Berkeley's.

are formed by *abstraction* in the manner premised; *universality,* so far as I can comprehend, not consisting in the absolute, positive nature or conception of anything, but in the relation it bears to the particulars signified or represented by it: by virtue whereof it is that things, names, or notions, being in their own nature *particular,* are rendered *universal.* Thus when I demonstrate any proposition concerning triangles, it is to be supposed that I have in view the universal idea of a triangle; which ought not to be understood as if I could frame an idea of a triangle which was neither equilateral nor scalenon nor equicrural. But only that the particular triangle I consider, whether of this or that sort it matters not, does equally stand for and represent all rectilinear triangles whatsoever, and is in that sense *universal.* All which seems very plain and not to include any difficulty in it.

16. But here it will be demanded, how we can know any proposition to be true of all particular triangles, except we have first seen it demonstrated of the abstract idea of a triangle which equally agrees to all? For because a property may be demonstrated to agree to some one particular triangle, it will not thence follow that it equally belongs to any other triangle, which in all respects is not the same with it. For example, having demonstrated that the three angles of an isosceles rectangular triangle are equal to two right ones, I cannot therefore conclude this affection agrees to all other triangles, which have neither a right angle, nor two equal sides. It seems therefore that, to be certain this proposition is universally true, we must either make a particular demonstration for every particular triangle, which is impossible, or once for all demonstrate it of the *abstract idea of a triangle,* in which all the particulars do indifferently partake, and by which they are all equally represented. To which I answer, that though the idea I have in view whilst I make the demonstration, be, for instance, that of an isosceles rectangular triangle, whose sides are of a determinate length, I may nevertheless be certain it extends to all other rectilinear triangles, of what sort or bigness soever. And that, because neither the right angle, nor the equality, nor determinate length of the sides, are at all concerned in the demonstration. It is true, the diagram I have in view includes all these particulars, but then there is not the least mention made of them in the proof of the proposition. It is not said, the three angles are equal to two right ones, because one of them is a right angle, or because the sides comprehending it are of the same length. Which sufficiently shows that the right angle might have been oblique, and the sides unequal, and for

all that the demonstration have held good. And for this reason it is, that I conclude that to be true of any obliquangular or scalenon, which I had demonstrated of a particular right-angled, equicrural triangle; and not because I demonstrated the proposition of the abstract idea of a triangle. [And here it must be acknowledged that a man may consider a figure merely as triangular, without attending to the particular qualities of the angles, or relations of the sides. So far he may abstract: but this will never prove, that he can frame an abstract general inconsistent idea of a triangle. In like manner we may consider *Peter* so far forth as man, or so far forth as animal, without framing the forementioned abstract idea, either of man or of animal, inasmuch as all that is perceived is not considered.][3]

17. It were an endless, as well as a useless thing, to trace the *Schoolmen*, those great masters of abstraction, through all the manifold inextricable labyrinths of error and dispute, which their doctrine of abstract natures and notions seems to have led them into.[4] What bickerings and controversies, and what a learned dust have been raised about those matters, and what mighty advantage has been from thence derived to mankind, are things at this day too clearly known to need being insisted on. And it had been well if the ill effects of that doctrine were confined to those only who make the most avowed profession of it. When men consider the great pains, industry and parts, that have for so many ages been laid out on the cultivation and advancement of the sciences, and that notwithstanding all this, the far greater part of them remain full of darkness and uncertainty, and disputes that are like never to have an end, and even those that are thought to be supported by the most clear and cogent demonstrations, contain in them paradoxes which are perfectly irreconcilable to the understandings of men, and that taking all together, a small portion of them does supply any real benefit to mankind, otherwise than by being an innocent diversion and amusement: I

---

3. The bracketed passage was added in the second edition.

4. "Schoolmen" refers to the philosophers and theologians who taught in the medieval universities (the "Schools") and to later figures who philosophized in their style. They were also known as "Scholastics." Berkeley does not refer to any of the Schoolmen by name in the *Principles*, but in *Alciphron* IV he briefly discusses St. Thomas Aquinas (c. 1224–1274) and Francisco Suarez (1548–1617). Berkeley's opinion of the Schoolmen is typical of its time: he thinks their "bickerings and controversies" are over-subtle and useless (a view expressed in the present section), and that they too often defer to the authority of Aristotle (see Introduction 20). For a brief account of scholastic views on abstraction, see Weinberg,."The Nominalism of Berkeley and Hume."

say, the consideration of all this is apt to throw them into a despondency, and perfect contempt of all study. But this may perhaps cease, upon a view of the false principles that have obtained in the world, amongst all which there is none, methinks, has a more wide influence over the thoughts of speculative men, than this of abstract general ideas.

18. I come now to consider the source of this prevailing notion, and that seems to me to be language. And surely nothing of less extent than reason itself could have been the source of an opinion so universally received. The truth of this appears as from other reasons, so also from the plain confession of the ablest patrons of abstract ideas, who acknowledge that they are made in order to naming; from which it is a clear consequence, that if there had been no such thing as speech or universal signs, there never had been any thought of abstraction. *See* B. 3. C. 6. Sect. 39. *and elsewhere of the Essay on Human Understanding.* Let us therefore examine the manner wherein words have contributed to the origin of that mistake. First then, 'tis thought that every name has, or ought to have, one only precise and settled signification, which inclines men to think there are certain *abstract, determinate ideas,* which constitute the true and only immediate signification of each general name. And that it is by the mediation of these abstract ideas, that a general name comes to signify any particular thing. Whereas, in truth, there is no such thing as one precise and definite signification annexed to any general name, they all signifying indifferently a great number of particular ideas. All which does evidently follow from what has been already said, and will clearly appear to anyone by a little reflection. To this it will be objected, that every name that has a definition, is thereby restrained to one certain signification. For example, a *triangle* is defined to be a *plain surface comprehended by three right lines;* by which that name is limited to denote one certain idea and no other. To which I answer, that in the definition it is not said whether the surface be great or small, black or white, nor whether the sides are long or short, equal or unequal, nor with what angles they are inclined to each other; in all which there may be great variety, and consequently there is no one settled idea which limits the signification of the word *triangle.* 'Tis one thing for to keep a name constantly to the same definition, and another to make it stand everywhere for the same idea: the one is necessary, the other useless and impracticable.

19. But to give a farther account how words came to produce the doctrine of abstract ideas, it must be observed that it is a received

opinion, that language has no other end but the communicating our ideas, and that every significant name stands for an idea. This being so, and it being withal certain, that names, which yet are not thought altogether insignificant, do not always mark out particular conceivable ideas, it is straightway concluded that they stand for abstract notions. That there are many names in use amongst speculative men, which do not always suggest to others determinate particular ideas, is what nobody will deny. And a little attention will discover, that it is not necessary (even in the strictest reasonings) significant names which stand for ideas should, every time they are used, excite in the understanding the ideas they are made to stand for: in reading and discoursing, names being for the most part used as letters are in *algebra*, in which though a particular quantity be marked by each letter, yet to proceed right it is not requisite that in every step each letter suggest to your thoughts, that particular quantity it was appointed to stand for.

20. Besides, the communicating of ideas marked by words is not the chief and only end of language, as is commonly supposed. There are other ends, as the raising of some passion, the exciting to, or deterring from an action, the putting the mind in some particular disposition; to which the former is in many cases barely subservient, and sometimes entirely omitted, when these can be obtained without it, as I think does not infrequently happen in the familiar use of language. I entreat the reader to reflect with himself, and see if it does not often happen either in hearing or reading a discourse, that the passions of fear, love, hatred, admiration, disdain, and the like, arise immediately in his mind upon the perception of certain words, without any ideas coming between. At first, indeed, the words might have occasioned ideas that were fit to produce those emotions; but, if I mistake not, it will be found that when language is once grown familiar, the hearing of the sounds or sight of the characters is oft immediately attended with those passions, which at first were wont to be produced by the intervention of ideas, that are now quite omitted. May we not, for example, be affected with the promise of a *good thing*, though we have not an idea of what it is? Or is not the being threatened with danger sufficient to excite a dread, though we think not of any particular evil likely to befall us, nor yet frame to ourselves an idea of danger in abstract? If anyone shall join ever so little reflection of his own to what has been said, I believe it will evidently appear to him, that general names are often used in the propriety of language without the speaker's designing them for marks of ideas in his own, which he

would have them raise in the mind of the hearer. Even proper names themselves do not seem always spoken, with a design to bring into our view the ideas of those individuals that are supposed to be marked by them. For example, when a Schoolman tells me *Aristotle has said it,* all I conceive he means by it, is to dispose me to embrace his opinion with the deference and submission which custom has annexed to that name. And this effect may be so instantly produced in the minds of those who are accustomed to resign their judgment to the authority of that philosopher, as it is impossible any idea either of his person, writings, or reputation should go before. Innumerable examples of this kind may be given, but why should I insist on those things, which everyone's experience will, I doubt not, plentifully suggest unto him?

21. We have, I think, shown the impossibility of *abstract ideas.* We have considered what has been said for them by their ablest patrons; and endeavored to show they are of no use for those ends, to which they are thought necessary. And lastly, we have traced them to the source from whence they flow, which appears to be language. It cannot be denied that words are of excellent use, in that by their means all that stock of knowledge which has been purchased by the joint labors of inquisitive men in all ages and nations, may be drawn into the view and made the possession of one single person. But at the same time it must be owned that most parts of knowledge have been strangely perplexed and darkened by the abuse of words, and general ways of speech wherein they are delivered. Since therefore words are so apt to impose on the understanding, whatever ideas I consider, I shall endeavor to take them bare and naked into my view, keeping out of my thoughts, so far as I am able, those names which long and constant use has so strictly united with them; from which I may expect to derive the following advantages.

22. First, I shall be sure to get clear of all controversies purely verbal; the springing up of which weeds in almost all the sciences has been a main hindrance to the growth of true and sound knowledge. Secondly, this seems to be a sure way to extricate myself out of that fine and subtle net of *abstract ideas,* which has so miserably perplexed and entangled the minds of men, and that with this peculiar circumstance, that by how much the finer and more curious was the wit of any man, by so much the deeper was he like to be ensnared, and faster held therein. Thirdly, so long as I confine my thoughts to my own ideas divested of words, I do not see how I can easily be mistaken. The objects I consider, I clearly and adequately know. I cannot be deceived in thinking I have an idea which

I have not. It is not possible for me to imagine, that any of my own ideas are alike or unlike, that are not truly so. To discern the agreements or disagreements there are between my ideas, to see what ideas are included in any compound idea, and what not, there is nothing more requisite, than an attentive perception of what passes in my own understanding.

23. But the attainment of all these advantages does presuppose an entire deliverance from the deception of words, which I dare hardly promise myself; so difficult a thing it is to dissolve a union so early begun, and confirmed by so long a habit as that betwixt words and ideas. Which difficulty seems to have been very much increased by the doctrine of *abstraction.* For so long as men thought abstract ideas were annexed to their words, it does not seem strange that they should use words for ideas: it being found an impracticable thing to lay aside the word, and retain the abstract idea in the mind, which in itself was perfectly inconceivable. This seems to me the principal cause, why those men who have so emphatically recommended to others, the laying aside all use of words in their meditations, and contemplating their bare ideas, have yet failed to perform it themselves.[5] Of late many have been very sensible of the absurd opinions and insignificant disputes, which grow out of the abuse of words. And in order to remedy these evils they advise well, that we attend to the ideas signified, and draw off our attention from the words which signify them. But how good soever this advice may be, they have given others, it is plain they could not have a due regard to it themselves, so long as they thought the only immediate use of words was to signify ideas, and that the immediate signification of every general name was a *determinate, abstract idea.*

24. But these being known to be mistakes, a man may with greater ease prevent his being imposed on by words. He that knows he has no other than particular ideas, will not puzzle himself in vain to find out and conceive the abstract idea, annexed to any name. And he that knows names do not always stand for ideas, will spare himself the labor of looking for ideas, where there are none to be had. It were therefore to be wished that everyone would use his utmost endeavors, to obtain a clear view of the ideas he would consider, separating from them all that dress and encumbrance of words which so much contribute to blind the

---

5. No doubt Berkeley is thinking of Locke, who often advises his readers to lay aside words and attend to ideas. See for example *Essay* IV iv 17 and IV iii 30.

judgment and divide the attention. In vain do we extend our view into the heavens, and pry into the entrails of the earth, in vain do we consult the writings of learned men, and trace the dark footsteps of antiquity; we need only draw the curtain of words, to behold the fairest tree of knowledge, whose fruit is excellent, and within the reach of our hand.

25. Unless we take care to clear the first principles of knowledge, from the embarras and delusion of words, we may make infinite reasonings upon them to no purpose; we may draw consequences from consequences, and be never the wiser. The farther we go, we shall only lose ourselves the more irrecoverably, and be the deeper entangled in difficulties and mistakes. Whoever therefore designs to read the following sheets, I entreat him to make my words the occasion of his own thinking, and endeavor to attain the same train of thoughts in reading, that I had in writing them. By this means it will be easy for him to discover the truth or falsity of what I say. He will be out of all danger of being deceived by my words, and I do not see how he can be led into an error by considering his own naked, undisguised ideas.

Of the

Principles

of

Human Knowledge.

Part I.[1]

1. It is evident to anyone who takes a survey of the objects of human knowledge, that they are either ideas actually imprinted on the senses, or else such as are perceived by attending to the passions and operations of the mind, or lastly ideas formed by help of memory and imagination, either compounding, dividing, or barely representing those originally perceived in the aforesaid ways. By sight I have the ideas of light and colors with their several degrees and variations. By touch I perceive, for example, hard and soft, heat and cold, motion and resistance, and of all these more and less either as to quantity or degree. Smelling furnishes me with odors; the palate with tastes, and hearing conveys sounds to the mind in all their variety of tone and composition. And as several of these are observed to accompany each other, they come to be marked by one name, and so to be reputed as one thing. Thus, for example, a certain color, taste, smell, figure and consistence having been observed to go together, are accounted one distinct thing, signified by the name *apple*. Other collections of ideas constitute a stone, a tree, a book, and the like sensible things; which, as they are pleasing or disagreeable, excite the passions of love, hatred, joy, grief, and so forth.

2. But besides all that endless variety of ideas or objects of knowledge, there is likewise something which knows or perceives them, and exercises divers operations, as willing, imagining, remembering about them. This perceiving, active being is what I call *mind*, *spirit*, *soul* or *myself*. By which words I do not denote any one of my ideas, but a thing entirely distinct from them, wherein they exist, or, which is the same thing, whereby they are perceived; for the existence of an idea consists in being perceived.

3. That neither our thoughts, nor passions, nor ideas formed by the imagination, exist without the mind, is what everybody will allow. And

1 Part II was never published. See the Editor's Introduction, p. xi.

it seems no less evident that the various sensations or ideas imprinted on the sense, however blended or combined together (that is, whatever objects they compose) cannot exist otherwise than in a mind perceiving them. I think an intuitive knowledge may be obtained of this, by anyone that shall attend to what is meant by the term *exist* when applied to sensible things. The table I write on, I say, exists, that is, I see and feel it; and if I were out of my study I should say it existed, meaning thereby that if I was in my study I might perceive it, or that some other spirit actually does perceive it. There was an odor, that is, it was smelled; there was a sound, that is to say, it was heard; a color or figure, and it was perceived by sight or touch. This is all that I can understand by these and the like expressions. For as to what is said of the absolute existence of unthinking things without any relation to their being perceived, that seems perfectly unintelligible. Their *esse* is *percipi*, nor is it possible they should have any existence, out of the minds or thinking things which perceive them.[2]

4. It is indeed an opinion strangely prevailing amongst men, that houses, mountains, rivers, and in a word all sensible objects have an existence natural or real, distinct from their being perceived by the understanding. But with how great an assurance and acquiescence soever this principle may be entertained in the world; yet whoever shall find in his heart to call it in question, may, if I mistake not, perceive it to involve a manifest contradiction. For what are the forementioned objects but the things we perceive by sense, and what do we perceive besides our own ideas or sensations; and is it not plainly repugnant that any one of these or any combination of them should exist unperceived?

5. If we thoroughly examine this tenet, it will, perhaps, be found at bottom to depend on the doctrine of *abstract ideas*. For can there be a nicer strain of abstraction than to distinguish the existence of sensible objects from their being perceived, so as to conceive them existing unperceived? Light and colors, heat and cold, extension and figures, in a word the things we see and feel, what are they but so many sensations, notions, ideas or impressions on the sense; and is it possible to separate, even in thought, any of these from perception? For my part I might as easily divide a thing from itself. I may indeed divide in my thoughts or conceive apart from each other those things which, perhaps, I never perceived by sense so divided. Thus I imagine the trunk of a human

2. *esse*, to be; *percipi*, to be perceived.

body without the limbs, or conceive the smell of a rose without thinking on the rose itself. So far I will not deny I can abstract, if that may properly be called *abstraction*, which extends only to the conceiving separately such objects, as it is possible may really exist or be actually perceived asunder. But my conceiving or imagining power does not extend beyond the possibility of real existence or perception. Hence as it is impossible for me to see or feel anything without an actual sensation of that thing, so is it impossible for me to conceive in my thoughts any sensible thing or object distinct from the sensation or perception of it.[3]

6. Some truths there are so near and obvious to the mind, that a man need only open his eyes to see them. Such I take this important one to be, to wit, that all the choir of heaven and furniture of the earth, in a word all those bodies which compose the mighty frame of the world, have not any subsistence without a mind, that their being is to be perceived or known; that consequently so long as they are not actually perceived by me, or do not exist in my mind or that of any other created spirit, they must either have no existence at all, or else subsist in the mind of some eternal spirit: it being perfectly unintelligible and involving all the absurdity of abstraction, to attribute to any single part of them an existence independent of a spirit. To be convinced of which, the reader need only reflect and try to separate in his own thoughts the being of a sensible thing from its being perceived.

7. From what has been said, it follows, there is not any other substance than *spirit*, or that which perceives. But for the fuller proof of this point, let it be considered, the sensible qualities are color, figure, motion, smell, taste, and such like, that is, the ideas perceived by sense. Now for an idea to exist in an unperceiving thing, is a manifest contradiction; for to have an idea is all one as to perceive: that therefore wherein color, figure, and the like qualities exist, must perceive them; hence it is clear there can be no unthinking substance or *substratum* of those ideas.

8. But say you, though the ideas themselves do not exist without the mind, yet there may be things like them whereof they are copies or resemblances, which things exist without the mind, in an unthinking substance. I answer, an idea can be like nothing but an idea; a color or figure can be like nothing but another color or figure. If we look but ever so little into our thoughts, we shall find it impossible for us to conceive a

---

3. In the first edition the section continues with the following sentence: *In truth the object and the sensation are the same thing, and cannot therefore be abstracted from each other.*

likeness except only between our ideas. Again, I ask whether those supposed originals or external things, of which our ideas are the pictures or representations, be themselves perceivable or no? If they are, then they are ideas, and we have gained our point; but if you say they are not, I appeal to anyone whether it be sense, to assert a color is like something which is invisible; hard or soft, like something which is intangible; and so of the rest.

9. Some there are who make a distinction betwixt *primary* and *secondary* qualities: by the former, they mean extension, figure, motion, rest, solidity or impenetrability and number: by the latter they denote all other sensible qualities, as colors, sounds, tastes, and so forth.[4] The ideas we have of these they acknowledge not to be the resemblances of anything existing without the mind or unperceived; but they will have our ideas of the primary qualities to be patterns or images of things which exist without the mind, in an unthinking substance which they call *matter*. By matter therefore we are to understand an inert, senseless substance, in which extension, figure, and motion, do actually subsist. But it is evident from what we have already shown, that extension, figure and motion are only ideas existing in the mind, and that an idea can be like nothing but another idea, and that consequently neither they nor their archetypes can exist in an unperceiving substance. Hence it is plain, that the very notion of what is called *matter* or *corporeal substance*, involves a contradiction in it.

10. They who assert that figure, motion, and the rest of the primary or original qualities do exist without the mind, in unthinking substances, do at the same time acknowledge that colors, sounds, heat, cold, and such like secondary qualities, do not, which they tell us are sensations existing in the mind alone, that depend on and are occasioned by the different size, texture and motion of the minute particles of matter. This they take for an undoubted truth, which they can demonstrate beyond all exception. Now if it be certain, that those original qualities are inseparably united with the other sensible qualities, and not, even in thought, capable of being abstracted from them, it plainly follows that they exist only in the mind. But I desire anyone to reflect and try, whether he can by any abstraction of thought, conceive the extension and motion of a body, without all other sensible qualities. For my own part, I see evidently that it is not in my power

4. Locke makes the distinction at *Essay* II viii 9–26.

to frame an idea of a body extended and moved, but I must withal give it some color or other sensible quality which is acknowledged to exist only in the mind. In short, extension, figure, and motion, abstracted from all other qualities, are inconceivable. Where therefore the other sensible qualities are, there must these be also, to wit, in the mind and nowhere else.

11. Again, *great* and *small*, *swift* and *slow*, are allowed to exist nowhere without the mind, being entirely relative, and changing as the frame or position of the organs of sense varies. The extension therefore which exists without the mind, is neither great nor small, the motion neither swift nor slow, that is, they are nothing at all. But say you, they are extension in general, and motion in general: thus we see how much the tenet of extended, moveable substances existing without the mind, depends on that strange doctrine of *abstract ideas*. And here I cannot but remark, how nearly the vague and indeterminate description of matter or corporeal substance, which the modern philosophers are run into by their own principles, resembles that antiquated and so much ridiculed notion of *materia prima*, to be met with in *Aristotle* and his followers.[5] Without extension solidity cannot be conceived; since therefore it has been shown that extension exists not in an unthinking substance, the same must also be true of solidity.

12. That number is entirely the creature of the mind, even though the other qualities be allowed to exist without, will be evident to whoever considers, that the same thing bears a different denomination of number, as the mind views it with different respects. Thus, the same extension is one or three or thirty six, according as the mind considers it with reference to a yard, a foot, or an inch. Number is so visibly relative, and dependent on men's understanding, that it is strange to think how anyone should give it an absolute existence without the mind. We say one book, one page, one line; all these are equally units, though some contain several of the others. And in each instance it is plain, the unit relates to some particular combination of ideas arbitrarily put together by the mind.

5. Aristotle (384–322 B.C.) calls the wood of a casket its *matter*. He thinks the various kinds of matter can be arranged in a hierarchy: wood, for example, is matter for a casket, while earth (one of the four basic elements) is matter for wood. *Materia prima*, or prime matter, is a totally indeterminate substratum, the most basic item in the hierarchy. Berkeley follows a long tradition when he attributes belief in prime matter to Aristotle, but it is a tradition many scholars now dispute.

13. Unity I know some will have to be a simple or uncompounded idea, accompanying all other ideas into the mind.[6] That I have any such idea answering the word *unity*, I do not find; and if I had, methinks I could not miss finding it; on the contrary it should be the most familiar to my understanding, since it is said to accompany all other ideas, and to be perceived by all the ways of sensation and reflection. To say no more, it is an *abstract idea*.

14. I shall farther add, that after the same manner, as modern philosophers prove certain sensible qualities to have no existence in matter, or without the mind, the same thing may be likewise proved of all other sensible qualities whatsoever. Thus, for instance, it is said that heat and cold are affections only of the mind, and not at all patterns of real beings, existing in the corporeal substances which excite them, for that the same body which appears cold to one hand, seems warm to another. Now why may we not as well argue that figure and extension are not patterns or resemblances of qualities existing in matter, because to the same eye at different stations, or eyes of a different texture at the same station, they appear various, and cannot therefore be the images of anything settled and determinate without the mind? Again, it is proved that sweetness is not really in the sapid thing, because the thing remaining unaltered the sweetness is changed into bitter, as in case of a fever or otherwise vitiated palate. Is it not as reasonable to say, that motion is not without the mind, since if the succession of ideas in the mind become swifter, the motion, it is acknowledged, shall appear slower without any alteration in any external object.

15. In short, let anyone consider those arguments, which are thought manifestly to prove that colors and tastes exist only in the mind, and he shall find they may with equal force, be brought to prove the same thing of extension, figure, and motion. Though it must be confessed this method of arguing does not so much prove that there is no extension or color in an outward object, as that we do not know by sense which is the true extension or color of the object. But the arguments foregoing plainly show it to be impossible that any color or extension at all, or other sensible quality whatsoever, should exist in an unthinking subject without the mind, or in truth, that there should be any such thing as an outward object.

16. But let us examine a little the received opinion. It is said extension is a mode or accident of matter, and that matter is the *substratum* that

6. Locke makes these observations about unity at *Essay* II xvi 1.

supports it. Now I desire that you would explain what is meant by matter's *supporting* extension: say you, I have no idea of matter, and therefore cannot explain it. I answer, though you have no positive, yet if you have any meaning at all, you must at least have a relative idea of matter; though you know not what it is, yet you must be supposed to know what relation it bears to accidents, and what is meant by its supporting them. It is evident *support* cannot here be taken in its usual or literal sense, as when we say that pillars support a building: in what sense therefore must it be taken?

17. If we inquire into what the most accurate philosophers declare themselves to mean by *material substance*; we shall find them acknowledge, they have no other meaning annexed to those sounds, but the idea of being in general, together with the relative notion of its supporting accidents.[7] The general idea of being appears to me the most abstract and incomprehensible of all other; and as for its supporting accidents, this, as we have just now observed, cannot be understood in the common sense of those words; it must therefore be taken in some other sense, but what that is they do not explain. So that when I consider the two parts or branches which make the signification of the words *material substance*, I am convinced there is no distinct meaning annexed to them. But why should we trouble ourselves any farther, in discussing this material *substratum* or support of figure and motion, and other sensible qualities? Does it not suppose they have an existence without the mind? And is not this a direct repugnancy, and altogether inconceivable?

18. But though it were possible that solid, figured, moveable substances may exist without the mind, corresponding to the ideas we have of bodies, yet how is it possible for us to know this? Either we must know it by sense, or by reason. As for our senses, by them we have the knowledge only of our sensations, ideas, or those things that are immediately perceived by sense, call them what you will: but they do not inform us that things exist without the mind, or unperceived, like to those which are perceived. This the materialists themselves acknowledge. It remains therefore that if we have any knowledge at all of external things, it must be by reason, inferring their existence from what is immediately perceived by sense. But what reason can induce us to believe the existence of

7. Berkeley is probably referring to Locke's remarks on "pure substance in general" at *Essay* II xxiii 2.

bodies without the mind, from what we perceive, since the very patrons of matter themselves do not pretend, there is any necessary connection betwixt them and our ideas? I say it is granted on all hands (and what happens in dreams, frenzies, and the like, puts it beyond dispute) that it is possible we might be affected with all the ideas we have now, though no bodies existed without, resembling them. Hence it is evident the supposition of external bodies is not necessary for the producing our ideas: since it is granted they are produced sometimes, and might possibly be produced always in the same order we see them in at present, without their concurrence.

19. But though we might possibly have all our sensations without them, yet perhaps it may be thought easier to conceive and explain the manner of their production, by supposing external bodies in their likeness rather than otherwise; and so it might be at least probable there are such things as bodies that excite their ideas in our minds. But neither can this be said; for though we give the materialists their external bodies, they by their own confession are never the nearer knowing how our ideas are produced: since they own themselves unable to comprehend in what manner body can act upon spirit, or how it is possible it should imprint any idea in the mind. Hence it is evident the production of ideas or sensations in our minds, can be no reason why we should suppose matter or corporeal substances, since that is acknowledged to remain equally inexplicable with, or without this supposition. If therefore it were possible for bodies to exist without the mind, yet to hold they do so, must needs be a very precarious opinion; since it is to suppose, without any reason at all, that God has created innumerable beings that are entirely useless, and serve to no manner of purpose.

20. In short, if there were external bodies, it is impossible we should ever come to know it; and if there were not, we might have the very same reasons to think there were that we have now. Suppose, what no one can deny possible, an intelligence, without the help of external bodies, to be affected with the same train of sensations or ideas that you are, imprinted in the same order and with like vividness in his mind. I ask whether that intelligence has not all the reason to believe the existence of corporeal substances, represented by his ideas, and exciting them in his mind, that you can possibly have for believing the same thing? Of this there can be no question; which one consideration is enough to make any reasonable person suspect the strength of whatever arguments he may think himself to have, for the existence of bodies without the mind.

21. Were it necessary to add any farther proof against the existence of matter, after what has been said, I could instance several of those errors and difficulties (not to mention impieties) which have sprung from that tenet. It has occasioned numberless controversies and disputes in philosophy, and not a few of far greater moment in religion. But I shall not enter into the detail of them in this place, as well because I think, arguments *a posteriori* are unnecessary for confirming what has been, if I mistake not, sufficiently demonstrated *a priori*, as because I shall hereafter find occasion to say somewhat of them.[8]

22. I am afraid I have given cause to think me needlessly prolix in handling this subject. For to what purpose is it to dilate on that which may be demonstrated with the utmost evidence in a line or two, to anyone that is capable of the least reflection? It is but looking into your own thoughts, and so trying whether you can conceive it possible for a sound, or figure, or motion, or color, to exist without the mind, or unperceived. This easy trial may make you see, that what you contend for, is a downright contradiction. Insomuch that I am content to put the whole upon this issue; if you can but conceive it possible for one extended moveable substance, or in general, for any one idea or anything like an idea, to exist otherwise than in a mind perceiving it, I shall readily give up the cause: and as for all that *compages* of external bodies which you contend for, I shall grant you its existence, though you cannot either give me any reason why you believe it exists, or assign any use to it when it is supposed to exist. I say, the bare possibility of your opinion's being true, shall pass for an argument that it is so.

23. But say you, surely there is nothing easier than to imagine trees, for instance, in a park, or books existing in a closet, and nobody by to perceive them. I answer, you may so, there is no difficulty in it: but what is all this, I beseech you, more than framing in your mind certain ideas

8. *a posteriori*, from what comes after; *a priori*, from what comes before. These are among the first appearances of these expressions in English. (They are the first appearances listed in the *Oxford English Dictionary*, but the expressions were used as early as 1679 in discussions of arguments for God's existence. See Redwood, *Reason, Ridicule and Religion*, pp. 151–52.) Berkeley does not use the expressions as philosophers do today. According to Berkeley, an *a posteriori* argument against a belief attacks the belief through its effects or consequences, which in the case of matter include skepticism, atheism, and various difficulties in physics and mathematics. An *a priori* argument attacks the belief directly. Berkeley's promise to present the *a posteriori* case against matter is fulfilled in sections 85–96 and 101–34.

which you call *books* and *trees*, and at the same time omitting to frame the idea of anyone that may perceive them? But do not you yourself perceive or think of them all the while? This therefore is nothing to the purpose: it only shows you have the power of imagining or forming ideas in your mind; but it does not show that you can conceive it possible, the objects of your thought may exist without the mind: to make out this, it is necessary that you conceive them existing unconceived or unthought of, which is a manifest repugnancy. When we do our utmost to conceive the existence of external bodies, we are all the while only contemplating our own ideas. But the mind taking no notice of itself, is deluded to think it can and does conceive bodies existing unthought of or without the mind; though at the same time they are apprehended by or exist in itself. A little attention will discover to anyone the truth and evidence of what is here said, and make it unnecessary to insist on any other proofs against the existence of material substance.

24. It is very obvious, upon the least inquiry into our own thoughts, to know whether it be possible for us to understand what is meant, by the *absolute existence of sensible objects in themselves, or without the mind*. To me it is evident those words mark out either a direct contradiction, or else nothing at all. And to convince others of this, I know no readier or fairer way, than to entreat they would calmly attend to their own thoughts: and if by this attention, the emptiness or repugnancy of those expressions does appear, surely nothing more is requisite for their conviction. It is on this therefore that I insist, to wit, that the absolute existence of unthinking things are words without a meaning, or which include a contradiction. This is what I repeat and inculcate, and earnestly recommend to the attentive thoughts of the reader.

25. All our ideas, sensations, or the things which we perceive, by whatsoever names they may be distinguished, are visibly inactive, there is nothing of power or agency included in them.[9] So that one idea or object of thought cannot produce, or make any alteration in another. To be satisfied of the truth of this, there is nothing else requisite but a bare observation of our ideas. For since they and every part of them exist only in the mind, it follows that there is nothing in them but what is perceived. But whoever shall attend to his ideas, whether of sense or

9. In the first edition, the word "notions" follows "sensations."

reflection, will not perceive in them any power or activity; there is therefore no such thing contained in them. A little attention will discover to us that the very being of an idea implies passiveness and inertness in it, insomuch that it is impossible for an idea to do anything, or, strictly speaking, to be the cause of anything: neither can it be the resemblance or pattern of any active being, as is evident from *Sect.* 8. Whence it plainly follows that extension, figure and motion, cannot be the cause of our sensations. To say therefore, that these are the effects of powers resulting from the configuration, number, motion, and size of corpuscles, must certainly be false.

26. We perceive a continual succession of ideas, some are anew excited, others are changed or totally disappear. There is therefore some cause of these ideas whereon they depend, and which produces and changes them. That this cause cannot be any quality or idea or combination of ideas, is clear from the preceding section. It must therefore be a substance; but it has been shown that there is no corporeal or material substance: it remains therefore that the cause of ideas is an incorporeal active substance or spirit.

27. A spirit is one simple, undivided, active being: as it perceives ideas, it is called the *understanding*, and as it produces or otherwise operates about them, it is called the *will*. Hence there can be no idea formed of a soul or spirit: for all ideas whatever, being passive and inert, *vide Sect.* 25, they cannot represent unto us, by way of image or likeness, that which acts. A little attention will make it plain to anyone, that to have an idea which shall be like that active principle of motion and change of ideas, is absolutely impossible. Such is the nature of *spirit* or that which acts, that it cannot be of itself perceived, but only by the effects which it produces. If any man shall doubt of the truth of what is here delivered, let him but reflect and try if he can frame the idea of any power or active being; and whether he has ideas of two principal powers, marked by the names *will* and *understanding*, distinct from each other as well as from a third idea of substance or being in general, with a relative notion of its supporting or being the subject of the aforesaid powers, which is signified by the name *soul* or *spirit*. This is what some hold; but so far as I can see, the words *will, soul, spirit*, do not stand for different ideas, or in truth, for any idea at all, but for something which is very different from ideas, and which being an agent cannot be like unto, or represented by, any idea whatsoever. [Though it must be owned at the same time, that we have some notion of soul, spirit, and the operations of the mind, such

as willing, loving, hating, inasmuch as we know or understand the meaning of those words.][10]

28. I find I can excite ideas in my mind at pleasure, and vary and shift the scene as oft as I think fit. It is no more than willing, and straightway this or that idea arises in my fancy: and by the same power it is obliterated, and makes way for another. This making and unmaking of ideas does very properly denominate the mind active. Thus much is certain, and grounded on experience: but when we talk of unthinking agents, or of exciting ideas exclusive of volition, we only amuse ourselves with words.

29. But whatever power I may have over my own thoughts, I find the ideas actually perceived by sense have not a like dependence on my will. When in broad daylight I open my eyes, it is not in my power to choose whether I shall see or no, or to determine what particular objects shall present themselves to my view; and so likewise as to the hearing and other senses, the ideas imprinted on them are not creatures of my will. There is therefore some other will or spirit that produces them.

30. The ideas of sense are more strong, lively, and distinct than those of the imagination; they have likewise a steadiness, order, and coherence, and are not excited at random, as those which are the effects of human wills often are, but in a regular train or series, the admirable connection whereof sufficiently testifies the wisdom and benevolence of its author. Now the set rules or established methods, wherein the mind we depend on excites in us the ideas of sense, are called the *laws of nature*: and these we learn by experience, which teaches us that such and such ideas are attended with such and such other ideas, in the ordinary course of things.

31. This gives us a sort of foresight, which enables us to regulate our actions for the benefit of life. And without this we should be eternally at a loss: we could not know how to act anything that might procure us the least pleasure, or remove the least pain of sense. That food nourishes, sleep refreshes, and fire warms us; that to sow in the seed-time is the way to reap in the harvest, and, in general, that to obtain such or such ends, such or such means are conducive, all this we know, not by discovering any necessary connection between our ideas, but only by the observation of the settled laws of nature, without which we should be all in

---

10. The bracketed sentence was added in the second edition.

uncertainty and confusion, and a grown man no more know how to manage himself in the affairs of life, than an infant just born.

32. And yet this consistent uniform working, which so evidently displays the goodness and wisdom of that governing spirit whose will constitutes the laws of nature, is so far from leading our thoughts to him, that it rather sends them awandering after second causes. For when we perceive certain ideas of sense constantly followed by other ideas, and we know this is not of our own doing, we forthwith attribute power and agency to the ideas themselves, and make one the cause of another, than which nothing can be more absurd and unintelligible. Thus, for example, having observed that when we perceive by sight a certain round luminous figure, we at the same time perceive by touch the idea or sensation called *heat*, we do from thence conclude the sun to be the cause of heat. And in like manner perceiving the motion and collision of bodies to be attended with sound, we are inclined to think the latter an effect of the former.

33. The ideas imprinted on the senses by the Author of Nature are called *real things:* and those excited in the imagination being less regular, vivid and constant, are more properly termed *ideas*, or *images of things*, which they copy and represent. But then our sensations, be they never so vivid and distinct, are nevertheless *ideas*, that is, they exist in the mind, or are perceived by it, as truly as the ideas of its own framing. The ideas of sense are allowed to have more reality in them, that is, to be more strong, orderly, and coherent than the creatures of the mind; but this is no argument that they exist without the mind. They are also less dependent on the spirit, or thinking substance which perceives them, in that they are excited by the will of another and more powerful spirit: yet still they are *ideas*, and certainly no *idea*, whether faint or strong, can exist otherwise than in a mind perceiving it.

34. Before we proceed any farther, it is necessary to spend some time in answering objections which may probably be made against the principles hitherto laid down. In doing of which, if I seem too prolix to those of quick apprehensions, I hope it may be pardoned, since all men do not equally apprehend things of this nature; and I am willing to be understood by everyone. First then, it will be objected that by the foregoing principles, all that is real and substantial in nature is banished out of the world: and instead thereof a chimerical scheme of ideas takes place. All things that exist, exist only in the mind, that is, they are purely

notional. What therefore becomes of the sun, moon, and stars? What must we think of houses, rivers, mountains, trees, stones; nay, even of our own bodies? Are all these but so many chimeras and illusions on the fancy? To all which, and whatever else of the same sort may be objected, I answer, that by the principles premised, we are not deprived of any one thing in nature. Whatever we see, feel, hear, or any wise conceive or understand, remains as secure as ever, and is as real as ever. There is a *rerum natura*, and the distinction between realities and chimeras retains its full force. This is evident from *Sect.* 29, 30, and 33, where we have shown what is meant by *real things* in opposition to *chimeras*, or ideas of our own framing; but then they both equally exist in the mind, and in that sense are alike *ideas*.

35. I do not argue against the existence of any one thing that we can apprehend, either by sense or reflection. That the things I see with mine eyes and touch with my hands do exist, really exist, I make not the least question. The only thing whose existence we deny, is that which philosophers call matter or corporeal substance. And in doing of this, there is no damage done to the rest of mankind, who, I dare say, will never miss it. The atheist indeed will want the color of an empty name to support his impiety; and the philosophers may possibly find, they have lost a great handle for trifling and disputation.

36. If any man thinks this detracts from the existence or reality of things, he is very far from understanding what has been premised in the plainest terms I could think of. Take here an abstract of what has been said. There are spiritual substances, minds, or human souls, which will or excite ideas in themselves at pleasure: but these are faint, weak, and unsteady in respect of others they perceive by sense, which being impressed upon them according to certain rules or laws of nature, speak themselves the effects of a mind more powerful and wise than human spirits. These latter are said to have more *reality* in them than the former: by which is meant that they are more affecting, orderly, and distinct, and that they are not fictions of the mind perceiving them. And in this sense, the sun that I see by day is the real sun, and that which I imagine by night is the idea of the former. In the sense here given of *reality*, it is evident that every vegetable, star, mineral, and in general each part of the mundane system, is as much a *real being* by our principles as by any other. Whether others mean anything by the term *reality* different from what I do, I entreat them to look into their own thoughts and see.

37. It will be urged that thus much at least is true, to wit, that we take away all corporeal substances. To this my answer is, that if the word *substance* be taken in the vulgar sense, for a combination of sensible qualities, such as extension, solidity, weight, and the like; this we cannot be accused of taking away. But if it be taken in a philosophic sense, for the support of accidents or qualities without the mind: then indeed I acknowledge that we take it away, if one may be said to take away that which never had any existence, not even in the imagination.

38. But, say you, it sounds very harsh to say we eat and drink ideas, and are clothed with ideas. I acknowledge it does so, the word *idea* not being used in common discourse to signify the several combinations of sensible qualities, which are called *things:* and it is certain that any expression which varies from the familiar use of language, will seem harsh and ridiculous. But this does not concern the truth of the proposition, which in other words is no more than to say, we are fed and clothed with those things which we perceive immediately by our senses. The hardness or softness, the color, taste, warmth, figure, and such like qualities, which combined together constitute the several sorts of victuals and apparel, have been shown to exist only in the mind that perceives them; and this is all that is meant by calling them *ideas*; which word, if it was as ordinarily used as *thing*, would sound no harsher nor more ridiculous than it. I am not for disputing about the propriety, but the truth of the expression. If therefore you agree with me that we eat and drink, and are clad with the immediate objects of sense which cannot exist unperceived or without the mind: I shall readily grant it is more proper or conformable to custom, that they should be called things rather than ideas.

39. If it be demanded why I make use of the word *idea*, and do not rather in compliance with custom call them things. I answer, I do it for two reasons: first, because the term *thing*, in contradistinction to *idea*, is generally supposed to denote somewhat existing without the mind: secondly, because *thing* has a more comprehensive signification than *idea*, including spirits or thinking things as well as ideas. Since therefore the objects of sense exist only in the mind, and are withal thoughtless and inactive, I chose to mark them by the word *idea*, which implies those properties.

40. But say what we can, someone perhaps may be apt to reply, he will still believe his senses, and never suffer any arguments, how plausible

soever, to prevail over the certainty of them. Be it so, assert the evidence of sense as high as you please, we are willing to do the same. That what I see, hear and feel does exist, that is to say, is perceived by me, I no more doubt than I do of my own being. But I do not see how the testimony of sense can be alleged, as a proof for the existence of anything, which is not perceived by sense. We are not for having any man turn *skeptic*, and disbelieve his senses; on the contrary we give them all the stress and assurance imaginable; nor are there any principles more opposite to skepticism, than those we have laid down, as shall be hereafter clearly shown.

41. Secondly, it will be objected that there is a great difference betwixt real fire, for instance, and the idea of fire, betwixt dreaming or imagining oneself burnt, and actually being so: this and the like may be urged in opposition to our tenets. To all which the answer is evident from what has been already said, and I shall only add in this place, that if real fire be very different from the idea of fire, so also is the real pain that it occasions, very different from the idea of the same pain: and yet nobody will pretend that real pain either is, or can possibly be, in an unperceiving thing or without the mind, any more than its idea.

42. Thirdly, it will be objected that we see things actually without or at a distance from us, and which consequently do not exist in the mind, it being absurd that those things which are seen at the distance of several miles, should be as near to us as our own thoughts. In answer to this, I desire it may be considered, that in a dream we do oft perceive things as existing at a great distance off, and yet for all that, those things are acknowledged to have their existence only in the mind.

43. But for the fuller clearing of this point, it may be worthwhile to consider, how it is that we perceive distance and things placed at a distance by sight. For that we should in truth see external space, and bodies actually existing in it, some nearer, others farther off, seems to carry with it some opposition to what has been said, of their existing nowhere without the mind. The consideration of this difficulty it was, that gave birth to my *Essay towards a New Theory of Vision*, which was published not long since. Wherein it is shown that *distance* or outness is neither immediately of itself perceived by sight, nor yet apprehended or judged of by lines and angles, or anything that has a necessary connection with it: but that it is only suggested to our thoughts, by certain visible ideas and sensations attending vision, which

in their own nature have no manner of similitude or relation, either with distance, or things placed at a distance.[11] But by a connection taught us by experience, they come to signify and suggest them to us, after the same manner that words of any language suggest the ideas they are made to stand for. Insomuch that a man born blind, and afterwards made to see, would not, at first sight, think the things he saw, to be without his mind, or at any distance from him. See *Sect.* 41. of the forementioned treatise.

44. The ideas of sight and touch make two species, entirely distinct and heterogeneous. The former are marks and prognostics of the latter. That the proper objects of sight neither exist without the mind, nor are the images of external things, was shown even in that treatise. Though throughout the same, the contrary be supposed true of tangible objects: not that to suppose that vulgar error, was necessary for establishing the notion therein laid down; but because it was beside my purpose to examine and refute it in a discourse concerning *vision*. So that in strict truth the ideas of sight, when we apprehend by them distance and things placed at a distance, do not suggest or mark out to us things actually existing at a distance, but only admonish us what ideas of touch will be imprinted in our minds at such and such distances of time, and in consequence of such or such actions. It is, I say, evident from what has been said in the foregoing parts of this treatise, and in *Sect.* 147, and elsewhere of the essay concerning vision, that visible ideas are the language whereby the governing spirit, on whom we depend, informs us what tangible ideas he is about to imprint upon us, in case we excite this or that motion in our own bodies. But for a fuller information in this point, I refer to the essay itself.

45. Fourthly, it will be objected that from the foregoing principles it follows, things are every moment annihilated and created anew. The objects of sense exist only when they are perceived: the trees therefore are in the garden, or the chairs in the parlor, no longer than while there is somebody by to perceive them. Upon shutting my eyes all the furniture in the room is reduced to nothing, and barely upon opening them it is again created. In answer to all which, I refer the reader to what has been said in *Sect.* 3, 4, etc. and desire he will consider whether he means anything by the actual existence of an idea, distinct from its being perceived. For my part, after the nicest inquiry I could make, I am not

---

11. For these arguments, see *An Essay towards a New Theory of Vision* 1–28.

able to discover that anything else is meant by those words. And I once more entreat the reader to sound his own thoughts, and not suffer himself to be imposed on by words. If he can conceive it possible either for his ideas or their archetypes to exist without being perceived, then I give up the cause: but if he cannot, he will acknowledge it is unreasonable for him to stand up in defense of he knows not what, and pretend to charge on me as an absurdity, the not assenting to those propositions which at bottom have no meaning in them.

46. It will not be amiss to observe, how far the received principles of philosophy are themselves chargeable with those pretended absurdities. It is thought strangely absurd that upon closing my eyelids, all the visible objects round me should be reduced to nothing; and yet is not this what philosophers commonly acknowledge, when they agree on all hands, that light and colors, which alone are the proper and immediate objects of sight, are mere sensations that exist no longer than they are perceived? Again, it may to some perhaps seem very incredible, that things should be every moment creating, yet this very notion is commonly taught in the Schools. For the *Schoolmen*, though they acknowledge the existence of matter, and that the whole mundane fabric is framed out of it, are nevertheless of opinion that it cannot subsist without the divine conservation, which by them is expounded to be a continual creation.

47. Farther, a little thought will discover to us, that though we allow the existence of matter or corporeal substance, yet it will unavoidably follow from the principles which are now generally admitted, that the particular bodies of what kind soever, do none of them exist whilst they are not perceived. For it is evident from *Sect.* 11. and the following sections, that the matter philosophers contend for, is an incomprehensible somewhat which has none of those particular qualities, whereby the bodies falling under our senses are distinguished one from another. But to make this more plain, it must be remarked, that the infinite divisibility of matter is now universally allowed, at least by the most approved and considerable philosophers, who on the received principles demonstrate it beyond all exception. Hence it follows, that there is an infinite number of parts in each particle of matter, which are not perceived by sense. The reason therefore, that any particular body seems to be of a finite magnitude, or exhibits only a finite number of parts to sense, is, not because it contains no more, since in itself it contains an infinite number of parts, but because the sense is not acute

enough to discern them. In proportion therefore as the sense is rendered more acute, it perceives a greater number of parts in the object, that is, the object appears greater, and its figure varies, those parts in its extremities which were before unperceivable, appearing now to bound it in very different lines and angles from those perceived by an obtuser sense. And at length, after various changes of size and shape, when the sense becomes infinitely acute, the body shall seem infinite. During all which there is no alteration in the body, but only in the sense. Each body therefore considered in itself, is infinitely extended, and consequently void of all shape or figure. From which it follows, that though we should grant the existence of matter to be ever so certain, yet it is withal as certain, the materialists themselves are by their own principles forced to acknowledge, that neither the particular bodies perceived by sense, nor anything like them exists without the mind. Matter, I say, and each particle thereof is according to them infinite and shapeless, and it is the mind that frames all that variety of bodies which compose the visible world, any one whereof does not exist longer than it is perceived.

48. If we consider it, the objection proposed in *Sect.* 45. will not be found reasonably charged on the principles we have premised, so as in truth to make any objection at all against our notions. For though we hold indeed the objects of sense to be nothing else but ideas which cannot exist unperceived; yet we may not hence conclude they have no existence except only while they are perceived by us, since there may be some other spirit that perceives them, though we do not. Wherever bodies are said to have no existence without the mind, I would not be understood to mean this or that particular mind, but all minds whatsoever. It does not therefore follow from the foregoing principles, that bodies are annihilated and created every moment, or exist not at all during the intervals between our perception of them.

49. Fifthly, it may perhaps be objected, that if extension and figure exist only in the mind, it follows that the mind is extended and figured; since extension is a mode or attribute, which (to speak with the Schools) is predicated of the subject in which it exists. I answer, those qualities are in the mind only as they are perceived by it, that is, not by way of *mode* or *attribute*, but only by way of *idea*; and it no more follows, that the soul or mind is extended because extension exists in it alone, than it does that it is red or blue, because those colors are on all hands acknowledged to exist in it, and nowhere else. As to what philosophers say of subject and mode, that seems very groundless and unintelligible. For instance, in

this proposition, a die is hard, extended and square, they will have it that the word *die* denotes a subject or substance, distinct from the hardness, extension and figure, which are predicated of it, and in which they exist. This I cannot comprehend: to me a die seems to be nothing distinct from those things which are termed its modes or accidents. And to say a die is hard, extended and square, is not to attribute those qualities to a subject distinct from and supporting them, but only an explication of the meaning of the word *die*.

50. Sixthly, you will say there have been a great many things explained by matter and motion: take away these, and you destroy the whole corpuscular philosophy, and undermine those mechanical principles which have been applied with so much success to account for the *phenomena*. In short, whatever advances have been made, either by ancient or modern philosophers, in the study of nature, do all proceed on the supposition, that corporeal substance or matter does really exist. To this I answer, that there is not any one *phenomenon* explained on that supposition, which may not as well be explained without it, as might easily be made appear by an induction of particulars. To explain the *phenomena*, is all one as to show, why upon such and such occasions we are affected with such and such ideas. But how matter should operate on a spirit, or produce any idea in it, is what no philosopher will pretend to explain. It is therefore evident, there can be no use of matter in natural philosophy. Besides, they who attempt to account for things, do it not by corporeal substance, but by figure, motion, and other qualities, which are in truth no more than mere ideas, and therefore cannot be the cause of anything, as has been already shown. See *Sect. 25*.

51. Seventhly, it will upon this be demanded whether it does not seem absurd to take away natural causes, and ascribe everything to the immediate operation of spirits? We must no longer say upon these principles that fire heats, or water cools, but that a spirit heats, and so forth. Would not a man be deservedly laughed at, who should talk after this manner? I answer, he would so; in such things we ought to *think with the learned, and speak with the vulgar*. They who to demonstration are convinced of the truth of the *Copernican* system, do nevertheless say the sun rises, the sun sets, or comes to the meridian: and if they affected a contrary style in common talk, it would without doubt appear very ridiculous. A little reflection on what is here said will make it manifest, that the common use of language would receive no manner of alteration or disturbance from the admission of our tenets.

52. In the ordinary affairs of life, any phrases may be retained, so long as they excite in us proper sentiments, or dispositions to act in such a manner as is necessary for our well-being, how false soever they may be, if taken in a strict and speculative sense. Nay this is unavoidable, since propriety being regulated by custom, language is suited to the received opinions, which are not always the truest. Hence it is impossible, even in the most rigid philosophic reasonings, so far to alter the bent and genius of the tongue we speak, as never to give a handle for cavillers to pretend difficulties and inconsistencies. But a fair and ingenuous reader will collect the sense, from the scope and tenor and connection of a discourse, making allowances for those inaccurate modes of speech, which use has made inevitable.

53. As to the opinion that there are no corporeal causes, this has been heretofore maintained by some of the Schoolmen, as it is of late by others among the modern philosophers, who though they allow matter to exist, yet will have God alone to be the immediate efficient cause of all things.[12] These men saw, that amongst all the objects of sense, there was none which had any power or activity included in it, and that by consequence this was likewise true of whatever bodies they supposed to exist without the mind, like unto the immediate objects of sense. But then, that they should suppose an innumerable multitude of created beings, which they acknowledge are not capable of producing any one effect in nature, and which therefore are made to no manner of purpose, since God might have done everything as well without them; this I say, though we should allow it possible, must yet be a very unaccountable and extravagant supposition.

54. In the eighth place, the universal concurrent assent of mankind may be thought by some, an invincible argument in behalf of matter, or the existence of external things. Must we suppose the whole world to be mistaken? And if so, what cause can be assigned of so widespread and predominant an error? I answer, first, that upon a narrow inquiry, it will not perhaps be found, so many as is imagined do really believe the existence of matter or things without the mind. Strictly speaking, to believe that which involves a contradiction, or has no meaning in it, is impossible: and whether the foregoing expressions are not of that sort, I refer it to the impartial examination of the reader. In one sense indeed,

12. One of the "modern philosophers" is Nicolas Malebranche (1638–1715). See his *The Search after Truth*, Book 6, Part 2, chapter 3.

men may be said to believe that matter exists, that is, they act as if the immediate cause of their sensations, which affects them every moment and is so nearly present to them, were some senseless unthinking being. But that they should clearly apprehend any meaning marked by those words, and form thereof a settled speculative opinion, is what I am not able to conceive. This is not the only instance wherein men impose upon themselves, by imagining they believe those propositions they have often heard, though at bottom they have no meaning in them.

55. But secondly, though we should grant a notion to be ever so universally and steadfastly adhered to, yet this is but a weak argument of its truth, to whoever considers what a vast number of prejudices and false opinions are everywhere embraced with the utmost tenaciousness, by the unreflecting (which are the far greater) part of mankind. There was a time when the *antipodes* and motion of the earth were looked upon as monstrous absurdities, even by men of learning: and if it be considered what a small proportion they bear to the rest of mankind, we shall find that at this day, those notions have gained but a very inconsiderable footing in the world.

56. But it is demanded, that we assign a cause of this prejudice, and account for its obtaining in the world. To this I answer, that men knowing they perceived several ideas, whereof they themselves were not the authors, as not being excited from within, nor depending on the operation of their wills, this made them maintain, those ideas or objects of perception had an existence independent of, and without the mind, without ever dreaming that a contradiction was involved in those words. But philosophers having plainly seen, that the immediate objects of perception do not exist without the mind, they in some degree corrected the mistake of the vulgar, but at the same time run into another which seems no less absurd, to wit, that there are certain objects really existing without the mind, or having a subsistence distinct from being perceived, of which our ideas are only images or resemblances, imprinted by those objects on the mind. And this notion of the philosophers owes its origin to the same cause with the former, namely, their being conscious that they were not the authors of their own sensations, which they evidently knew were imprinted from without, and which therefore must have some cause, distinct from the minds on which they are imprinted.

57. But why they should suppose the ideas of sense to be excited in us by things in their likeness, and not rather have recourse to *spirit* which

alone can act, may be accounted for, first, because they were not aware of the repugnancy there is, as well in supposing things like unto our ideas existing without, as in attributing to them power or activity. Secondly, because the supreme spirit which excites those ideas in our minds, is not marked out and limited to our view by any particular finite collection of sensible ideas, as human agents are by their size, complexion, limbs, and motions. And thirdly, because his operations are regular and uniform. Whenever the course of nature is interrupted by a miracle, men are ready to own the presence of a superior agent. But when we see things go on in the ordinary course, they do not excite in us any reflection; their order and concatenation, though it be an argument of the greatest wisdom, power, and goodness in their creator, is yet so constant and familiar to us, that we do not think them the immediate effects of a *free spirit*: especially since inconstancy and mutability in acting, though it be an imperfection, is looked on as a mark of *freedom*.

58. Tenthly, it will be objected, that the notions we advance, are inconsistent with several sound truths in philosophy and mathematics. For example, the motion of the earth is now universally admitted by astronomers, as a truth grounded on the clearest and most convincing reasons; but on the foregoing principles, there can be no such thing. For motion being only an idea, it follows that if it be not perceived, it exists not; but the motion of the earth is not perceived by sense. I answer, that tenet, if rightly understood, will be found to agree with the principles we have premised: for the question, whether the earth moves or no, amounts in reality to no more than this, to wit, whether we have reason to conclude from what has been observed by astronomers, that if we were placed in such and such circumstances, and such or such a position and distance, both from the earth and sun, we should perceive the former to move among the choir of the planets, and appearing in all respects like one of them: and this, by the established rules of nature, which we have no reason to mistrust, is reasonably collected from the phenomena.

59. We may, from the experience we have had of the train and succession of ideas in our minds, often make, I will not say uncertain conjectures, but sure and well-grounded predictions, concerning the ideas we shall be affected with, pursuant to a great train of actions, and be enabled to pass a right judgment of what would have appeared to us, in case we were placed in circumstances very different from those we are in at present. Herein consists the knowledge of nature, which may

preserve its use and certainty very consistently with what has been said. It will be easy to apply this to whatever objections of the like sort may be drawn from the magnitude of the stars, or any other discoveries in astronomy or nature.

60. In the eleventh place, it will be demanded to what purpose serves that curious organization of plants, and the admirable mechanism in the parts of animals; might not vegetables grow, and shoot forth leaves and blossoms, and animals perform all their motions, as well without as with all that variety of internal parts so elegantly contrived and put together, which being ideas have nothing powerful or operative in them, nor have any necessary connection with the effects ascribed to them? If it be a spirit that immediately produces every effect by a *fiat*, or act of his will, we must think all that is fine and artificial in the works, whether of man or nature, to be made in vain. By this doctrine, though an artist has made the spring and wheels, and every movement of a watch, and adjusted them in such a manner as he knew would produce the motions he designed; yet he must think all this done to no purpose, and that it is an intelligence which directs the index, and points to the hour of the day. If so, why may not the intelligence do it, without his being at the pains of making the movements, and putting them together? Why does not an empty case serve as well as another? And how comes it to pass, that whenever there is any fault in the going of a watch, there is some corresponding disorder to be found in the movements, which being mended by a skillful hand, all is right again? The like may be said of all the clockwork of nature, great part whereof is so wonderfully fine and subtle, as scarce to be discerned by the best microscope. In short, it will be asked, how upon our principles any tolerable account can be given, or any final cause assigned of an innumerable multitude of bodies and machines framed with the most exquisite art, which in the common philosophy have very apposite uses assigned them, and serve to explain abundance of phenomena.

61. To all which I answer, first, that though there were some difficulties relating to the administration of providence, and the uses by it assigned to the several parts of nature, which I could not solve by the foregoing principles, yet this objection could be of small weight against the truth and certainty of those things which may be proved *a priori*, with the utmost evidence. Secondly, but neither are the received principles free from the like difficulties; for it may still be demanded, to what end God should take those roundabout methods of effecting things by instru-

ments and machines, which no one can deny might have been effected by the mere command of his will, without all that *apparatus:* nay, if we narrowly consider it, we shall find the objection may be retorted with greater force on those who hold the existence of those machines without the mind; for it has been made evident, that solidity, bulk, figure, motion and the like, have no *activity* or *efficacy* in them, so as to be capable of producing any one effect in nature. See *Sect.* 25. Whoever therefore supposes them to exist (allowing the supposition possible) when they are not perceived, does it manifestly to no purpose; since the only use that is assigned to them, as they exist unperceived, is that they produce those perceivable effects, which in truth cannot be ascribed to anything but spirit.

62. But to come nearer the difficulty, it must be observed, that though the fabrication of all those parts and organs be not absolutely necessary to the producing any effect, yet it is necessary to the producing of things in a constant, regular way, according to the laws of nature. There are certain general laws that run through the whole chain of natural effects: these are learned by the observation and study of nature, and are by men applied as well to the framing artificial things for the use and ornament of life, as to the explaining the various *phenomena*: which explication consists only in showing the conformity any particular phenomenon has to the general laws of nature, or, which is the same thing, in discovering the *uniformity* there is in the production of natural effects; as will be evident to whoever shall attend to the several instances, wherein philosophers pretend to account for appearances. That there is a great and conspicuous use in these regular constant methods of working observed by the Supreme Agent, has been shown in *Sect.* 31. And it is no less visible, that a particular size, figure, motion and disposition of parts are necessary, though not absolutely to the producing any effect, yet to the producing it according to the standing mechanical laws of nature. Thus, for instance, it cannot be denied that God, or the intelligence which sustains and rules the ordinary course of things might, if he were minded to produce a miracle, cause all the motions on the dial-plate of a watch, though nobody had ever made the movements, and put them in it: but yet if he will act agreeably to the rules of mechanism, by him for wise ends established and maintained in the creation, it is necessary that those actions of the watchmaker, whereby he makes the movements and rightly adjusts them, precede the production of the aforesaid motions; as also that any disorder in them be attended with the perception

of some corresponding disorder in the movements, which being once corrected all is right again.

63. It may indeed on some occasions be necessary, that the Author of Nature display his overruling power in producing some appearance out of the ordinary series of things. Such exceptions from the general rules of nature are proper to surprise and awe men into an acknowledgment of the Divine Being: but then they are to be used but seldom, otherwise there is a plain reason why they should fail of that effect. Besides, God seems to choose the convincing our reason of his attributes by the works of nature, which discover so much harmony and contrivance in their make, and are such plain indications of wisdom and beneficence in their author, rather than to astonish us into a belief of his being by anomalous and surprising events.

64. To set this matter in a yet clearer light, I shall observe that what has been objected in *Sect.* 60. amounts in reality to no more than this: ideas are not anyhow and at random produced, there being a certain order and connection between them, like to that of cause and effect: there are also several combinations of them, made in a very regular and artificial manner, which seem like so many instruments in the hand of nature, that being hid as it were behind the scenes, have a secret operation in producing those appearances which are seen on the theater of the world, being themselves discernible only to the curious eye of the philosopher. But since one idea cannot be the cause of another, to what purpose is that connection? And since those instruments, being barely *inefficacious perceptions* in the mind, are not subservient to the production of natural effects; it is demanded why they are made, or, in other words, what reason can be assigned why God should make us, upon a close inspection into his works, behold so great variety of ideas, so artfully laid together, and so much according to rule; it not being credible, that he would be at the expense (if one may so speak) of all that art and regularity to no purpose?

65. To all which my answer is, first, that the connection of ideas does not imply the relation of *cause* and *effect*, but only of a mark or *sign* with the thing *signified*. The fire which I see is not the cause of the pain I suffer upon my approaching it, but the mark that forewarns me of it. In like manner, the noise that I hear is not the effect of this or that motion or collision of the ambient bodies, but the sign thereof. Secondly, the reason why ideas are formed into machines, that is, artificial and regular

combinations, is the same with that for combining letters into words. That a few original ideas may be made to signify a great number of effects and actions, it is necessary they be variously combined together: and to the end their use be permanent and universal, these combinations must be made by *rule*, and with *wise contrivance*. By this means abundance of information is conveyed unto us, concerning what we are to expect from such and such actions, and what methods are proper to be taken, for the exciting such and such ideas: which in effect is all that I conceive to be distinctly meant, when it is said that by discerning the figure, texture, and mechanism of the inward parts of bodies, whether natural or artificial, we may attain to know the several uses and properties depending thereon, or the nature of the thing.

66. Hence it is evident, that those things which under the notion of a cause cooperating or concurring to the production of effects, are altogether inexplicable, and run us into great absurdities, may be very naturally explained, and have a proper and obvious use assigned them, when they are considered only as marks or signs for our information. And it is the searching after, and endeavoring to understand those signs instituted by the Author of Nature, that ought to be the employment of the natural philosopher, and not the pretending to explain things by corporeal causes; which doctrine seems to have too much estranged the minds of men from that active principle, that supreme and wise spirit, *in whom we live, move, and have our being.*[13]

67. In the twelfth place, it may perhaps be objected, that though it be clear from what has been said, that there can be no such thing as an inert, senseless, extended, solid, figured, moveable substance, existing without the mind, such as philosophers describe matter: yet if any man shall leave out of his idea of *matter*, the positive ideas of extension, figure, solidity and motion, and say that he means only by that word, an inert senseless substance, that exists without the mind, or unperceived, which is the occasion of our ideas, or at the presence whereof God is pleased to excite ideas in us: it does not appear, but that matter taken in this sense may possibly exist. In answer to which I say, first, that it seems no less absurd to suppose a substance without accidents, than it is to suppose accidents without a substance. But secondly, though we should grant this unknown substance may possibly exist, yet where can it be supposed to be? That it exists not in the mind is

13. Acts 17:28.

agreed, and that it exists not in place is no less certain; since all extension exists only in the mind, as has been already proved. It remains therefore that it exists nowhere at all.

68. Let us examine a little the description that is here given us of *matter*. It neither acts, nor perceives, nor is perceived: for this is all that is meant by saying it is an inert, senseless, unknown substance; which is a definition entirely made up of negatives, excepting only the relative notion of its standing under or supporting: but then it must be observed, that it *supports* nothing at all; and how nearly this comes to the description of a *non-entity*, I desire may be considered. But, say you, it is the *unknown occasion*, at the presence of which, ideas are excited in us by the will of God. Now I would fain know how anything can be present to us, which is neither perceivable by sense nor reflection, nor capable of producing any idea in our minds, nor is at all extended, nor has any form, nor exists in any place. The words *to be present*, when thus applied, must needs be taken in some abstract and strange meaning, and which I am not able to comprehend.

69. Again, let us examine what is meant by *occasion:* so far as I can gather from the common use of language, that word signifies, either the agent which produces any effect, or else something that is observed to accompany, or go before it, in the ordinary course of things. But when it is applied to matter as above described, it can be taken in neither of those senses. For matter is said to be passive and inert, and so cannot be an agent or efficient cause. It is also unperceivable, as being devoid of all sensible qualities, and so cannot be the occasion of our perceptions in the latter sense: as when the burning my finger is said to be the occasion of the pain that attends it. What therefore can be meant by calling matter an *occasion*? This term is either used in no sense at all, or else in some sense very distant from its received signification.

70. You will perhaps say that matter, though it be not perceived by us, is nevertheless perceived by God, to whom it is the occasion of exciting ideas in our minds. For, say you, since we observe our sensations to be imprinted in an orderly and constant manner, it is but reasonable to suppose there are certain constant and regular occasions of their being produced. That is to say, that there are certain permanent and distinct parcels of matter, corresponding to our ideas, which, though they do not excite them in our minds, or any ways immediately affect us, as being altogether passive and unperceivable to us, they are nevertheless to God,

by whom they are perceived, as it were so many occasions to remind him when and what ideas to imprint on our minds: that so things may go on in a constant uniform manner.

71. In answer to this I observe, that as the notion of matter is here stated, the question is no longer concerning the existence of a thing distinct from *spirit* and *idea*, from perceiving and being perceived: but whether there are not certain ideas, of I know not what sort, in the mind of God, which are so many marks or notes that direct him how to produce sensations in our minds, in a constant and regular method: much after the same manner as a musician is directed by the notes of music to produce that harmonious train and composition of sound, which is called a *tune*; though they who hear the music do not perceive the notes, and may be entirely ignorant of them. But this notion of matter seems too extravagant to deserve a confutation. Besides, it is in effect no objection against what we have advanced, to wit, that there is no senseless, unperceived *substance*.

72. If we follow the light of reason, we shall, from the constant uniform method of our sensations, collect the goodness and wisdom of the *spirit* who excites them in our minds. But this is all that I can see reasonably concluded from thence. To me, I say, it is evident that the being of a *spirit infinitely wise, good, and powerful* is abundantly sufficient to explain all the appearances of nature. But as for *inert senseless matter*, nothing that I perceive has any the least connection with it, or leads to the thoughts of it. And I would fain see anyone explain any the meanest *phenomenon* in nature by it, or show any manner of reason, though in the lowest rank of probability, that he can have for its existence; or even make any tolerable sense or meaning of that supposition. For as to its being an occasion, we have, I think, evidently shown that with regard to us it is no occasion: it remains therefore that it must be, if at all, the occasion to God of exciting ideas in us; and what this amounts to, we have just now seen.

73. It is worthwhile to reflect a little on the motives which induced men to suppose the existence of material substance; that so having observed the gradual ceasing, and expiration of those motives or reasons, we may proportionably withdraw the assent that was grounded on them. First therefore, it was thought that color, figure, motion, and the rest of the sensible qualities or accidents, did really exist without the mind; and for this reason, it seemed needful to suppose some unthinking *substratum* or *substance* wherein they did exist, since they could not be conceived to

exist by themselves. Afterwards, in process of time, men being convinced that colors, sounds, and the rest of the sensible secondary qualities had no existence without the mind, they stripped this *substratum* or material substance of those qualities, leaving only the primary ones, figure, motion, and such like, which they still conceived to exist without the mind, and consequently to stand in need of a material support. But it having been shown, that none, even of these, can possibly exist otherwise than in a spirit or mind which perceives them, it follows that we have no longer any reason to suppose the being of *matter*. Nay, that it is utterly impossible there should be any such thing, so long as that word is taken to denote an *unthinking substratum* of qualities or accidents, wherein they exist without the mind.

74. But though it be allowed by the *materialists* themselves, that matter was thought of only for the sake of supporting accidents; and the reason entirely ceasing, one might expect the mind should naturally, and without any reluctance at all, quit the belief of what was solely grounded thereon. Yet the prejudice is riveted so deeply in our thoughts, that we can scarce tell how to part with it, and are therefore inclined, since the *thing* itself is indefensible, at least to retain the *name*; which we apply to I know not what abstracted and indefinite notions of *being*, or *occasion*, though without any show of reason, at least so far as I can see. For what is there on our part, or what do we perceive amongst all the ideas, sensations, notions, which are imprinted on our minds, either by sense or reflection, from whence may be inferred the existence of an inert, thoughtless, unperceived occasion? And on the other hand, on the part of an *all-sufficient spirit*, what can there be that should make us believe, or even suspect, he is *directed* by an inert occasion to excite ideas in our minds?

75. It is a very extraordinary instance of the force of prejudice, and much to be lamented, that the mind of man retains so great a fondness against all the evidence of reason, for a stupid thoughtless *somewhat*, by the interposition whereof it would, as it were, screen itself from the providence of God, and remove him farther off from the affairs of the world. But though we do the utmost we can, to secure the belief of *matter*, though when reason forsakes us, we endeavor to support our opinion on the bare possibility of the thing, and though we indulge ourselves in the full scope of an imagination not regulated by reason, to make out that poor *possibility*, yet the upshot of all is, that there are certain *unknown ideas* in the mind of God; for this, if anything, is all

that I conceive to be meant by *occasion* with regard to God. And this, at the bottom, is no longer contending for the *thing*, but for the *name*.

76. Whether therefore there are such ideas in the mind of God, and whether they may be called by the name *matter*, I shall not dispute. But if you stick to the notion of an unthinking substance, or support of extension, motion, and other sensible qualities, then to me it is most evidently impossible there should be any such thing. Since it is a plain repugnancy, that those qualities should exist in or be supported by an unperceiving substance.

77. But say you, though it be granted that there is no thoughtless support of extension, and the other qualities or accidents which we perceive; yet there may, perhaps, be some inert unperceiving substance, or *substratum* of some other qualities, as incomprehensible to us as colors are to a man born blind, because we have not a sense adapted to them. But if we had a new sense, we should possibly no more doubt of their existence, than a blind man made to see does of the existence of light and colors. I answer, first, if what you mean by the word *matter* be only the unknown support of unknown qualities, it is no matter whether there is such a thing or no, since it no way concerns us: and I do not see the advantage there is in disputing about we know not *what*, and we know not *why*.

78. But secondly, if we had a new sense, it could only furnish us with new ideas or sensations: and then we should have the same reason against their existing in an unperceiving substance, that has been already offered with relation to figure, motion, color, and the like. Qualities, as has been shown, are nothing else but *sensations* or *ideas*, which exist only in a *mind* perceiving them; and this is true not only of the ideas we are acquainted with at present, but likewise of all possible ideas whatsoever.

79. But you will insist, what if I have no reason to believe the existence of matter, what if I cannot assign any use to it, or explain anything by it, or even conceive what is meant by that word? Yet still it is no contradiction to say that matter exists, and that this matter is *in general* a *substance*, or *occasion of ideas*; though, indeed, to go about to unfold the meaning, or adhere to any particular explication of those words, may be attended with great difficulties. I answer, when words are used without a meaning, you may put them together as you please, without danger of running into a contradiction. You may say, for example, that *twice two* is

equal to *seven*, so long as you declare you do not take the words of that proposition in their usual acceptation, but for marks of you know not what. And by the same reason you may say, there is an inert thoughtless substance without accidents, which is the occasion of our ideas. And we shall understand just as much by one proposition, as the other.

80. In the last place, you will say, what if we give up the cause of material substance, and assert, that matter is an unknown *somewhat*, neither substance nor accident, spirit nor idea, inert, thoughtless, indivisible, immoveable, unextended, existing in no place? For, say you, whatever may be urged against *substance* or *occasion*, or any other positive or relative notion of matter, has no place at all, so long as the *negative* definition of matter is adhered to. I answer, you may, if so it shall seem good, use the word *matter* in the same sense, that other men use *nothing*, and so make those terms convertible in your style. For after all, this is what appears to me to be the result of that definition, the parts whereof when I consider with attention, either collectively, or separate from each other, I do not find that there is any kind of effect or impression made on my mind, different from what is excited by the term *nothing*.

81. You will reply perhaps, that in the foresaid definition is included, what does sufficiently distinguish it from nothing, the positive abstract idea of *quiddity*, *entity*, or *existence*. I own indeed, that those who pretend to the faculty of framing abstract general ideas, do talk as if they had such an idea, which is, say they, the most abstract and general notion of all, that is to me the most incomprehensible of all others. That there are a great variety of spirits of different orders and capacities, whose faculties, both in number and extent, are far exceeding those the author of my being has bestowed on me, I see no reason to deny. And for me to pretend to determine by my own few, stinted, narrow inlets of perception, what ideas the inexhaustible power of the Supreme Spirit may imprint upon them, were certainly the utmost folly and presumption. Since there may be, for ought that I know, innumerable sorts of ideas or sensations, as different from one another, and from all that I have perceived, as colors are from sounds. But how ready soever I may be, to acknowledge the scantiness of my comprehension, with regard to the endless variety of spirits and ideas, that might possibly exist, yet for anyone to pretend to a notion of entity or existence, *abstracted* from *spirit* and *idea*, from perceiving and being perceived, is, I suspect, a downright repugnancy and trifling with words. It remains that we consider the objections, which may possibly be made on the part of religion.

82. Some there are who think, that though the arguments for the real existence of bodies, which are drawn from reason, be allowed not to amount to demonstration, yet the Holy Scriptures are so clear in the point, as will sufficiently convince every good Christian, that bodies do really exist, and are something more than mere ideas; there being in Holy Writ innumerable facts related, which evidently suppose the reality of timber, and stone, mountains, and rivers, and cities, and human bodies. To which I answer, that no sort of writings whatever, sacred or profane, which use those and the like words in the vulgar acceptation, or so as to have a meaning in them, are in danger of having their truth called in question by our doctrine. That all those things do really exist, that there are bodies, even corporeal substances, when taken in the vulgar sense, has been shown to be agreeable to our principles: and the difference betwixt *things* and *ideas*, *realities* and *chimeras*, has been distinctly explained.* And I do not think, that either what philosophers call *matter*, or the existence of objects without the mind, is anywhere mentioned in Scripture.

83. Again, whether there be, or be not external things, it is agreed on all hands, that the proper use of words, is the marking our conceptions, or things only as they are known and perceived by us; whence it plainly follows, that in the tenets we have laid down, there is nothing inconsistent with the right use and significancy of *language*, and that discourse of what kind soever, so far as it is intelligible, remains undisturbed. But all this seems so manifest, from what has been set forth in the premises, that it is needless to insist any farther on it.

84. But it will be urged, that miracles do, at least, lose much of their stress and import by our principles. What must we think of *Moses's* rod, was it not *really* turned into a serpent, or was there only a change of *ideas* in the minds of the spectators? And can it be supposed, that our Savior did no more at the marriage-feast in *Cana*, than impose on the sight, and smell, and taste of the guests, so as to create in them the appearance or idea only of wine? The same may be said of all other miracles: which, in consequence of the foregoing principles, must be looked upon only as so many cheats, or illusions of fancy. To this I reply, that the rod was changed into a real serpent, and the water into real wine. That this does not, in the least, contradict what I have elsewhere said, will be evident from *Sect.* 34, and 35. But this business of *real* and *imaginary* has been

*Sect. 29, 30, 33, 36, etc.

already so plainly and fully explained, and so often referred to, and the difficulties about it are so easily answered from what has gone before, that it were an affront to the reader's understanding, to resume the explication of it in this place. I shall only observe, that if at table all who were present should see, and smell, and taste, and drink wine, and find the effects of it, with me there could be no doubt of its reality. So that, at bottom, the scruple concerning real miracles has no place at all on ours, but only on the received principles, and consequently makes rather *for*, than *against* what has been said.

85. Having done with the objections, which I endeavored to propose in the clearest light, and gave them all the force and weight I could, we proceed in the next place to take a view of our tenets in their consequences. Some of these appear at first sight, as that several difficult and obscure questions, on which abundance of speculation has been thrown away, are entirely banished from philosophy. Whether corporeal substance can think? Whether matter be infinitely divisible? And how it operates on spirit? These and the like inquiries have given infinite amusement to philosophers in all ages. But depending on the existence of *matter*, they have no longer any place on our principles. Many other advantages there are, as well with regard to *religion* as the *sciences*, which it is easy for anyone to deduce from what has been premised. But this will appear more plainly in the sequel.

86. From the principles we have laid down, it follows, human knowledge may naturally be reduced to two heads, that of *ideas*, and that of *spirits*. Of each of these I shall treat in order. And first as to ideas or unthinking things, our knowledge of these has been very much obscured and confounded, and we have been led into very dangerous errors, by supposing a twofold existence of the objects of sense, the one *intelligible*, or in the mind, the other *real* and without the mind: whereby unthinking things are thought to have a natural subsistence of their own, distinct from being perceived by spirits. This which, if I mistake not, has been shown to be a most groundless and absurd notion, is the very root of *skepticism*; for so long as men thought that real things subsisted without the mind, and that their knowledge was only so far forth *real* as it was comfortable to *real things*, it follows, they could not be certain that they had any real knowledge at all. For how can it be known, that the things which are perceived, are conformable to those which are not perceived, or exist without the mind?

87. Color, figure, motion, extension and the like, considered only as so many *sensations* in the mind, are perfectly known, there being nothing in them which is not perceived. But if they are looked on as notes or images, referred to *things* or *archetypes* existing without the mind, then are we involved all in *skepticism*. We see only the appearances, and not the real qualities of things. What may be the extension, figure, or motion of anything really and absolutely, or in itself, it is impossible for us to know, but only the proportion or the relation they bear to our senses. Things remaining the same, our ideas vary, and which of them, or even whether any of them at all represent the true quality really existing in the thing, it is out of our reach to determine. So that, for ought we know, all we see, hear, and feel, may be only phantom and vain chimera, and not at all agree with the real things, existing in *rerum natura*. All this skepticism follows, from our supposing a difference between *things* and *ideas*, and that the former have a subsistence without the mind, or unperceived. It were easy to dilate on this subject, and show how the arguments urged by *skeptics* in all ages, depend on the supposition of external objects.

88. So long as we attribute a real existence to unthinking things, distinct from their being perceived, it is not only impossible for us to know with evidence the nature of any real unthinking being, but even that it exists. Hence it is, that we see philosophers distrust their senses, and doubt of the existence of heaven and earth, of everything they see or feel, even of their own bodies. And after all their labor and struggle of thought, they are forced to own, we cannot attain to any self-evident or demonstrative knowledge of the existence of sensible things.[14] But all this doubtfulness, which so bewilders and confounds the mind, and makes *philosophy* ridiculous in the eyes of the world, vanishes, if we annex a meaning to our words, and do not amuse ourselves with the terms *absolute, external, exist,* and such like, signifying we know not what. I can as well doubt of my own being, as of the being of those things which I actually perceive by sense: it being a manifest contradiction, that any sensible object should be immediately perceived by sight or touch, and at the same time have no existence in nature, since the very existence of an unthinking being consists in *being perceived*.

89. Nothing seems of more importance, towards erecting a firm system of sound and real knowledge, which may be proof against the assaults of

---

14. Locke denies we can have either self-evident or demonstrative knowledge of the existence of sensible things at *Essay* IV ii 14.

skepticism, than to lay the beginning in a distinct explication of what is meant by *thing, reality, existence:* for in vain shall we dispute concerning the real existence of things, or pretend to any knowledge thereof, so long as we have not fixed the meaning of those words. *Thing* or *being* is the most general name of all, it comprehends under it two kinds entirely distinct and heterogeneous, and which have nothing common but the name, to wit, *spirits* and *ideas.* The former are *active, indivisible substances:* the latter are *inert, fleeting, dependent beings,* which subsist not by themselves, but are supported by, or exist in minds or spiritual substances. [We comprehend our own existence by inward feeling or reflection, and that of other spirits by reason. We may be said to have some knowledge or notion of our own minds, of spirits and active beings, whereof in a strict sense we have not ideas. In like manner we know and have a notion of relations between things or ideas, which relations are distinct from the ideas or things related, inasmuch as the latter may be perceived by us without our perceiving the former. To me it seems that ideas, spirits and relations are all in their respective kinds, the object of human knowledge and subject of discourse: and that the term *idea* would be improperly extended to signify everything we know or have any notion of.][15]

90. Ideas imprinted on the senses are real things, or do really exist; this we do not deny, but we deny they can subsist without the minds which perceive them, or that they are resemblances of any archetypes existing without the mind: since the very being of a sensation or idea consists in being perceived, and an idea can be like nothing but an idea. Again, the things perceived by sense may be termed *external,* with regard to their origin, in that they are not generated from within, by the mind itself, but imprinted by a spirit distinct from that which perceives them. Sensible objects may likewise be said to be without the mind, in another sense, namely when they exist in some other mind. Thus when I shut my eyes, the things I saw may still exist, but it must be in another mind.

91. It were a mistake to think, that what is here said derogates in the least from the reality of things. It is acknowledged on the received principles, that extension, motion, and in a word all sensible qualities, have need of a support, as not being able to subsist by themselves. But the objects perceived by sense, are allowed to be nothing but combinations of those qualities, and consequently cannot subsist by themselves. Thus far it is

---

15. The bracketed passage was added in the second edition.

agreed on all hands. So that in denying the things perceived by sense, an existence independent of a substance, or support wherein they may exist, we detract nothing from the received opinion of their *reality*, and are guilty of no innovation in that respect. All the difference is, that according to us the unthinking beings perceived by sense, have no existence distinct from being perceived, and cannot therefore exist in any other substance, than those unextended, indivisible substances, or *spirits*, which act, and think, and perceive them: whereas philosophers vulgarly hold, that the sensible qualities exist in an inert, extended, unperceiving substance, which they call *matter*, to which they attribute a natural subsistence, exterior to all thinking beings, or distinct from being perceived by any mind whatsoever, even the eternal mind of the Creator, wherein they suppose only ideas of the corporeal substances created by him: if indeed they allow them to be at all created.

92. For as we have shown the doctrine of matter or corporeal substance, to have been the main pillar and support of *skepticism*, so likewise upon the same foundation have been raised all the impious schemes of *atheism* and irreligion. Nay so great a difficulty has it been thought, to conceive matter produced out of nothing, that the most celebrated among the ancient philosophers, even of these who maintained the being of a God, have thought matter to be uncreated and coeternal with him. How great a friend material substance has been to *atheists* in all ages, were needless to relate. All their monstrous systems have so visible and necessary a dependence on it, that when this cornerstone is once removed, the whole fabric cannot choose but fall to the ground; insomuch that it is no longer worthwhile, to bestow a particular consideration on the absurdities of every wretched sect of *atheists*.

93. That impious and profane persons should readily fall in with those systems which favor their inclinations, by deriding immaterial substance, and supposing the soul to be divisible and subject to corruption as the body; which exclude all freedom, intelligence, and design from the formation of things, and instead thereof make a self-existent, stupid, unthinking substance the root and origin of all beings. That they should hearken to those who deny a providence, or inspection of a superior mind over the affairs of the world, attributing the whole series of events either to blind chance or fatal necessity, arising from the impulse of one body on another. All this is very natural. And on the other hand, when men of better principles observe the enemies of religion lay so great a stress on *unthinking matter*, and all of them use so

much industry and artifice to reduce everything to it; methinks they should rejoice to see them deprived of their grand support, and driven from that only fortress, without which your *Epicureans*, *Hobbists*, and the like, have not even the shadow of a pretense, but become the most cheap and easy triumph in the world.[16]

94. The existence of matter, or bodies unperceived, has not only been the main support of *atheists* and *fatalists*, but on the same principle does *idolatry* likewise in all its various forms depend. Did men but consider that the sun, moon, and stars, and every other object of the senses, are only so many sensations in their minds, which have no other existence but barely being perceived, doubtless they would never fall down, and worship their own *ideas*; but rather address their homage to that Eternal Invisible Mind which produces and sustains all things.

95. The same absurd principle, by mingling itself with the articles of our faith, has occasioned no small difficulties to Christians. For example, about the *resurrection*, how many scruples and objections have been raised by *Socinians* and others?[17] But do not the most plausible of them depend on the supposition, that a body is denominated the *same*, with regard not to the form or that which is perceived by sense, but the material substance which remains the same under several forms? Take away this *material substance*, about the identity whereof all the dispute is, and mean by *body* what every plain ordinary person means by that word, to wit, that which is immediately seen and felt, which is only a combination of sensible qualities, or ideas: and then their most unanswerable objections come to nothing.

96. Matter being once expelled out of nature, drags with it so many skeptical and impious notions, such an incredible number of disputes and puzzling questions, which have been thorns in the sides of divines,

---

16. Epicurus (341-270 B.C.) and Thomas Hobbes (1588-1679) both maintain that the universe is nothing but matter in motion. Epicurus acknowledges the existence of gods, but he believes they have no interest in the world. Hobbes writes as if he believes in God, and even offers a proof of God's existence, but he has always been suspected of atheism, in part because his metaphysics commits him to the view that God, if he exists, is a material thing.

17. The Socinians were followers of Fausto Sozzini (Latinized "Socinus," 1539-1604), and forerunners of the Unitarians. Though they denied the divinity of Christ, their leading catechism affirms the resurrection. In Berkeley's day the word "Socinian" was often applied to anyone who challenged Christian orthodoxy, and this probably explains Berkeley's use of it here. ˙

as well as philosophers, and made so much fruitless work for mankind; that if the arguments we have produced against it, are not found equal to demonstration (as to me they evidently seem) yet I am sure all friends to knowledge, peace, and religion, have reason to wish they were.

97. Beside the external existence of the objects of perception, another great source of errors and difficulties, with regard to ideal knowledge, is the doctrine of *abstract ideas*, such as it has been set forth in the Introduction. The plainest things in the world, those we are most intimately acquainted with, and perfectly know, when they are considered in an abstract way, appear strangely difficult and incomprehensible. Time, place, and motion, taken in particular or concrete, are what everybody knows; but having passed through the hands of a metaphysician, they become too abstract and fine, to be apprehended by men of ordinary sense. Bid your servant meet you at such a *time*, in such a *place*, and he shall never stay to deliberate on the meaning of those words: in conceiving that particular time and place, or the motion by which he is to get thither, he finds not the least difficulty. But if *time* be taken, exclusive of all those particular actions and ideas that diversify the day, merely for the continuation of existence, or duration in abstract, then it will perhaps gravel even a philosopher to comprehend it.

98. Whenever I attempt to frame a simple idea of *time*, abstracted from the succession of ideas in my mind, which flows uniformly, and is participated by all beings, I am lost and embrangled in inextricable difficulties. I have no notion of it at all, only I hear others say, it is infinitely divisible, and speak of it in such a manner as leads me to entertain odd thoughts of my existence: since that doctrine lays one under an absolute necessity of thinking, either that he passes away innumerable ages without a thought, or else that he is annihilated every moment of his life: both which seem equally absurd. Time therefore being nothing, abstracted from the succession of ideas in our minds, it follows that the duration of any finite spirit must be estimated by the number of ideas or actions succeeding each other in that same spirit or mind. Hence it is a plain consequence that the soul always thinks: and in truth whoever shall go about to divide in his thoughts, or abstract the *existence* of a spirit from its *cogitation*, will, I believe, find it no easy task.

99. So likewise, when we attempt to abstract extension and motion from all other qualities, and consider them by themselves, we presently lose sight of them, and run into great extravagancies. All which depend on a

twofold abstraction: first, it is supposed that extension, for example, may be abstracted from all other sensible qualities; and secondly, that the entity of extension may be abstracted from its being perceived. But whoever shall reflect, and take care to understand what he says, will, if I mistake not, acknowledge that all sensible qualities are alike *sensations*, and alike *real*; that where the extension is, there is the color too, to wit, in his mind, and that their archetypes can exist only in some other *mind*: and that the objects of sense are nothing but those sensations combined, blended, or (if one may so speak) concreted together: none of all which can be supposed to exist unperceived.

100. What it is for a man to be happy, or an object good, everyone may think he knows. But to frame an abstract idea of *happiness*, prescinded from all particular pleasure, or of *goodness*, from everything that is good, this is what few can pretend to. So likewise, a man may be just and virtuous, without having precise ideas of *justice* and *virtue*. The opinion that those and the like words stand for general notions abstracted from all particular persons and actions, seems to have rendered morality difficult, and the study thereof of less use to mankind. And in effect, the doctrine of *abstraction* has not a little contributed towards spoiling the most useful parts of knowledge.[18]

101. The two great provinces of speculative science, conversant about ideas received from sense and their relations, are *natural philosophy* and *mathematics*; with regard to each of these I shall make some observations. And first, I shall say somewhat of natural philosophy. On this subject it is, that the *skeptics* triumph: all that stock of arguments they produce to depreciate our faculties, and make mankind appear ignorant and low, are drawn principally from this head, to wit, that we are under an invincible blindness as to the *true* and *real* nature of things. This they exaggerate, and love to enlarge on. We are miserably bantered, say they, by our senses, and amused only with the outside and show of things. The real essence, the internal qualities, and constitution of every the meanest object, is hid from our view; something there is in every drop of water, every grain of sand, which it is beyond the power of human understanding to fathom or comprehend. But it is

18. In the first edition, the final sentence is replaced by following: *And, in effect, one may make a great progress in* School-ethics, *without ever being the wiser or better man for it, or knowing how to behave himself in the affairs of life, more to the advantage of himself, or his neighbors, than he did before. This hint may suffice, to let anyone see, the doctrine of* abstraction, *has not a little contributed, towards spoiling the most useful parts of knowledge.*

evident from what has been shown, that all this complaint is groundless, and that we are influenced by false principles to that degree as to mistrust our senses, and think we know nothing of those things which we perfectly comprehend.

102. One great inducement to our pronouncing ourselves ignorant of the nature of things, is the current opinion that everything includes within itself the cause of its properties: or that there is in each object an inward essence, which is the source whence its discernible qualities flow, and whereon they depend. Some have pretended to account for appearances by occult qualities, but of late they are mostly resolved into mechanical causes, to wit, the figure, motion, weight, and such like qualities of insensible particles: whereas in truth, there is no other agent or efficient cause than *spirit*, it being evident that motion, as well as all other *ideas*, is perfectly inert. See *Sect.* 25. Hence, to endeavor to explain the production of colors or sounds, by figure, motion, magnitude and the like, must needs be labor in vain. And accordingly, we see the attempts of that kind are not at all satisfactory. Which may be said, in general, of those instances, wherein one idea or quality is assigned for the cause of another. I need not say, how many *hypotheses* and speculations are left out, and how much the study of nature is abridged by this doctrine.

103. The great mechanical principle now in vogue is *attraction*. That a stone falls to the earth, or the sea swells towards the moon, may to some appear sufficiently explained thereby. But how are we enlightened by being told this is done by attraction? Is it that that word signifies the manner of the tendency, and that it is by the mutual drawing of bodies, instead of their being impelled or protruded towards each other? But nothing is determined of the manner of action, and it may as truly (for ought we know) be termed *impulse* or *protrusion* as *attraction*. Again, the parts of steel we see cohere firmly together, and this also is accounted for by attraction; but in this, as in the other instances, I do not perceive that anything is signified besides the effect itself; for as to the manner of the action whereby it is produced, or the cause which produces it, these are not so much as aimed at.

104. Indeed, if we take a view of the several *phenomena*, and compare them together, we may observe some likeness and conformity between them. For example, in the falling of a stone to the ground, in the rising of the sea towards the moon, in cohesion and crystallization, there is something alike, namely a union or mutual approach of bodies. So that

any one of these or the like *phenomena*, may not seem strange or surprising to a man who has nicely observed and compared the effects of nature. For that only is thought so which is uncommon, or a thing by itself, and out of the ordinary course of our observation. That bodies should tend towards the center of the earth, is not thought strange, because it is what we perceive every moment of our lives. But that they should have a like gravitation towards the center of the moon, may seem odd and unaccountable to most men, because it is discerned only in the tides. But a philosopher, whose thoughts take in a larger compass of nature, having observed a certain similitude of appearances, as well in the heavens as the earth, that argue innumerable bodies to have a mutual tendency towards each other, which he denotes by the general name *attraction*, whatever can be reduced to that, he thinks justly accounted for. Thus he explains the tides by the attraction of the terraqueous globe towards the moon, which to him does not appear odd or anomalous, but only a particular example of a general rule or law of nature.

105. If therefore we consider the difference there is betwixt natural philosophers and other men, with regard to their knowledge of the *phenomena*, we shall find it consists, not in an exacter knowledge of the efficient cause that produces them, for that can be no other than the *will of a spirit*, but only in a greater largeness of comprehension, whereby analogies, harmonies, and agreements are discovered in the works of nature, and the particular effects explained, that is, reduced to general rules, see *Sect.* 62, which rules grounded on the analogy, and uniformness observed in the production of natural effects, are most agreeable, and sought after by the mind; for that they extend our prospect beyond what is present, and near to us, and enable us to make very probable conjectures, touching things that may have happened at very great distances of time and place, as well as to predict things to come; which sort of endeavor towards omniscience, is much affected by the mind.

106. But we should proceed warily in such things: for we are apt to lay too great a stress on analogies, and to the prejudice of truth, humor that eagerness of the mind, whereby it is carried to extend its knowledge into general theorems. For example, gravitation, or mutual attraction, because it appears in many instances, some are straightway for pronouncing *universal*; and that to *attract, and be attracted by every other body, is an essential quality inherent in all bodies whatsoever*. Whereas it appears the fixed stars have no such tendency towards each other: and so far is that

gravitation, from being *essential* to bodies, that, in some instances a quite contrary principle seems to show itself: as in the perpendicular growth of plants, and the elasticity of the air. There is nothing necessary or essential in the case, but it depends entirely on the will of the *governing spirit*, who causes certain bodies to cleave together, or tend towards each other, according to various laws, whilst he keeps others at a fixed distance; and to some he gives a quite contrary tendency to fly asunder, just as he sees convenient.

107. After what has been premised, I think we may lay down the following conclusions. First, it is plain philosophers amuse themselves in vain, when they inquire for any natural efficient cause, distinct from a *mind* or *spirit*. Secondly, considering the whole creation is the workmanship of a *wise and good agent*, it should seem to become philosophers, to employ their thoughts (contrary to what some hold) about the final causes of things: and I must confess, I see no reason, why pointing out the various ends, to which natural things are adapted, and for which they were originally with unspeakable wisdom contrived, should not be thought one good way of accounting for them, and altogether worthy a philosopher.[19] Thirdly, from what has been premised no reason can be drawn, why the history of nature should not still be studied, and observations and experiments made, which, that they are of use to mankind, and enable us to draw any general conclusions, is not the result of any immutable habitudes, or relations between things themselves, but only of God's goodness and kindness to men in the administration of the world. See *Sect.* 30 and 31. Fourthly, by a diligent observation of the *phenomena* within our view, we may discover the general laws of nature, and from them deduce the other *phenomena*, I do not say *demonstrate*; for all deductions of that kind depend on a supposition that the Author of Nature always operates uniformly, and in a constant observance of those rules we take for principles: which we cannot evidently know.

108. Those men who frame general rules from the *phenomena*, and afterwards derive the *phenomena* from those rules, seem to consider signs rather than causes. A man may well understand natural signs without knowing their analogy, or being able to say by what rule a thing

19. Among the philosophers who deny either the existence of final causes or the propriety of inquiry into them are René Descartes (1596-1650), in *The Principles of Philosophy*, Part I, xxviii, and Baruch Spinoza (1632-1677), in the Appendix to Part I of his *Ethics*. On final and efficient causation, see the Editor's Introduction, pp. xxvii-xxviii.

is so or so. And as it is very possible to write improperly, through too strict an observance of general grammar-rules: so in arguing from general rules of nature, it is not impossible we may extend the analogy too far, and by that means run into mistakes.

109. As in reading other books, a wise man will choose to fix his thoughts on the sense and apply it to use, rather than lay them out in grammatical remarks on the language; so in perusing the volume of nature, it seems beneath the dignity of the mind to affect an exactness in reducing each particular *phenomenon* to general rules, or showing how it follows from them. We should propose to ourselves nobler views, such as to recreate and exalt the mind, with a prospect of the beauty, order, extent, and variety of natural things: hence, by proper inferences, to enlarge our notions of the grandeur, wisdom, and beneficence of the Creator: and lastly, to make the several parts of the creation, so far as in us lies, subservient to the ends they were designed for, God's glory, and the sustentation and comfort of our selves and fellow-creatures.

110. The best key for the aforesaid analogy, or natural science, will be easily acknowledged to be a certain celebrated treatise of *mechanics:* in the entrance of which justly admired treatise, time, space and motion, are distinguished into *absolute* and *relative, true* and *apparent, mathematical* and *vulgar:* which distinction, as it is at large explained by the author, does suppose those quantities to have an existence without the mind: and that they are ordinarily conceived with relation to sensible things, to which nevertheless in their own nature, they bear no relation at all.[20]

111. As for *time,* as it is there taken in an absolute or abstracted sense, for the duration or perseverance of the existence of things, I have nothing more to add concerning it, after what has been already said on that subject, *Sect.* 97 and 98. For the rest, this celebrated author holds there is an *absolute space,* which, being unperceivable to sense, remains in itself similar and immoveable: and relative space to be the measure thereof, which being moveable, and defined by its situation in respect of sensible bodies, is vulgarly taken for immoveable space. *Place* he defines to be that part of space which is occupied by any body. And according as the space is absolute or relative, so also is the place. *Absolute motion* is said to be the translation of a body from absolute place to

20. The treatise is *Mathematical Principles of Natural Philosophy,* published by Isaac Newton (1642–1727) in 1687. Berkeley refers to it under its Latin title in section 114.

absolute place, as relative motion is from one relative place to another. And because the parts of absolute space, do not fall under our senses, instead of them we are obliged to use their sensible measures: and so define both place and motion with respect to bodies, which we regard as immoveable. But it is said, in philosophical matters we must abstract from our senses, since it may be, that none of those bodies which seem to be quiescent, are truly so: and the same thing which is moved relatively, may be really at rest. As likewise one and the same body may be in relative rest and motion, or even moved with contrary relative motions at the same time, according as its place is variously defined. All which ambiguity is to be found in the apparent motions, but not at all in the true or absolute, which should therefore be alone regarded in philosophy. And the true, we are told, are distinguished from the apparent or relative motions by the following properties. First, in true or absolute motion, all parts which preserve the same position with respect to the whole, partake of the motions of the whole. Secondly, the place being moved, that which is placed therein is also moved: so that a body moving in a place which is in motion, does participate the motion of its place. Thirdly, true motion is never generated or changed, otherwise than by force impressed on the body itself. Fourthly, true motion is always changed by force impressed on the body moved. Fifthly, in circular motion barely relative, there is no centrifugal force, which nevertheless in that which is true or absolute, is proportional to the quantity of motion.

112. But notwithstanding what has been said, it does not appear to me, that there can be any motion other than *relative*: so that to conceive motion, there must be at least conceived two bodies, whereof the distance or position in regard to each other is varied. Hence if there was one only body in being, it could not possibly be moved. This seems evident, in that the idea I have of motion does necessarily include relation.

113. But though in every motion it be necessary to conceive more bodies than one, yet it may be that one only is moved, namely that on which the force causing the change of distance is impressed, or in other words, that to which the action is applied. For however some may define relative motion, so as to term that body *moved*, which changes its distance from some other body, whether the force or action causing that change were applied to it, or no: yet as relative motion is that which is perceived by sense, and regarded in the ordinary affairs of life, it should seem that

every man of common sense knows what it is, as well as the best philosopher: now I ask anyone, whether in his sense of motion as he walks along the streets, the stones he passes over may be said to *move*, because they change distance with his feet? To me it seems, that though motion includes a relation of one thing to another, yet it is not necessary that each term of relation be denominated from it. As a man may think of somewhat which does not think, so a body may be moved to or from another body, which is not therefore itself in motion.

114. As the place happens to be variously defined, the motion which is related to it varies. A man in a ship may be said to be quiescent, with relation to the sides of the vessel, and yet move with relation to the land. Or he may move eastward in respect of the one, and westward in respect of the other. In the common affairs of life, men never go beyond the earth to define the place of any body: and what is quiescent in respect of that, is accounted *absolutely* to be so. But philosophers who have a greater extent of thought, and juster notions of the system of things, discover even the earth itself to be moved. In order therefore to fix their notions, they seem to conceive the corporeal world as finite, and the utmost unmoved walls or shell thereof to be the place, whereby they estimate true motions. If we sound our own conceptions, I believe we may find all the absolute motion we can frame an idea of, to be at bottom no other than relative motion thus defined. For as has been already observed, absolute motion exclusive of all external relation is incomprehensible: and to this kind of relative motion, all the above-mentioned properties, causes, and effects ascribed to absolute motion, will, if I mistake not, be found to agree. As to what is said of the centrifugal force, that it does not at all belong to circular relative motion: I do not see how this follows from the experiment which is brought to prove it. See *Philosophiae Naturalis Principia Mathematica, in Schol. Def.* VIII. For the water in the vessel, at that time wherein it is said to have the greatest relative circular motion, has, I think, no motion at all: as is plain from the foregoing section.

115. For to denominate a body *moved*, it is requisite, first, that it change its distance or situation with regard to some other body: and secondly, that the force or action occasioning that change be applied to it. If either of these be wanting, I do not think that agreeably to the sense of mankind, or the propriety of language, a body can be said to be in motion. I grant indeed, that it is possible for us to think a body, which we see change its distance from some other, to be moved, though it have

no force applied to it, (in which sense there may be apparent motion,) but then it is, because the force causing the change of distance, is imagined by us to be applied or impressed on that body thought to move. Which indeed shows we are capable of mistaking a thing to be in motion which is not, and that is all.

116. From what has been said, it follows that the philosophic consideration of motion does not imply the being of an *absolute space*, distinct from that which is perceived by sense, and related to bodies: which that it cannot exist without the mind, is clear upon the same principles, that demonstrate the like of all other objects of sense. And perhaps, if we inquire narrowly, we shall find we cannot even frame an idea of *pure space*, exclusive of all body. This I must confess seems impossible, as being a most abstract idea. When I excite a motion in some part of my body, if it be free or without resistance, I say there is *space:* but if I find a resistance, then I say there is *body:* and in proportion as the resistance to motion is lesser or greater, I say the *space* is more or less *pure*. So that when I speak of pure or empty space, it is not to be supposed, that the word *space* stands for an idea distinct from, or conceivable without body and motion. Though indeed we are apt to think every noun substantive stands for a distinct idea, that may be separated from all others: which has occasioned infinite mistakes. When therefore supposing all the world to be annihilated besides my own body, I say there still remains *pure space:* thereby nothing else is meant, but only that I conceive it possible, for the limbs of my body to be moved on all sides without the least resistance: but if that too were annihilated, then there could be no motion, and consequently no space. Some perhaps may think the sense of seeing does furnish them with the idea of pure space; but it is plain from what we have elsewhere shown, that the ideas of space and distance are not obtained by that sense. See the *Essay concerning Vision.*[21]

117. What is here laid down, seems to put an end to all those disputes and difficulties, which have sprung up amongst the learned concerning the nature of *pure space*. But the chief advantage arising from it, is, that we are freed from that dangerous *dilemma*, to which several who have employed their thoughts on this subject, imagine themselves reduced, to wit, of thinking either that real space is God, or else that there is something beside God which is eternal, uncreated, infinite, indivisible, immutable. Both which may justly be thought pernicious and absurd

21. For distance, see *Theory of Vision* 1–28; for pure space, *Theory of Vision* 126.

notions. It is certain that not a few divines, as well as philosophers of great note, have, from the difficulty they found in conceiving either limits or annihilation of space, concluded it must be *divine*. And some of late have set themselves particularly to show, that the incommunicable attributes of God agree to it. Which doctrine, how unworthy soever it may seem of the divine nature, yet I do not see how we can get clear of it, so long as we adhere to the received opinions.

118. Hitherto of natural philosophy: we come now to make some inquiry concerning that other great branch of speculative knowledge, to wit, *mathematics*. These, how celebrated soever they may be, for their clearness and certainty of demonstration, which is hardly anywhere else to be found, cannot nevertheless be supposed altogether free from mistakes; if in their principles there lurks some secret error, which is common to the professors of those sciences with the rest of mankind. Mathematicians, though they deduce their theorems from a great height of evidence, yet their first principles are limited by the consideration of quantity: and they do not ascend into any inquiry concerning those transcendental maxims, which influence all the particular sciences, each part whereof, mathematics not excepted, does consequently participate of the errors involved in them. That the principles laid down by mathematicians are true, and their way of deduction from those principles clear and incontestable, we do not deny. But we hold, there may be certain erroneous maxims of greater extent than the object of mathematics, and for that reason not expressly mentioned, though tacitly supposed throughout the whole progress of that science; and that the ill effects of those secret unexamined errors are diffused through all the branches thereof. To be plain, we suspect the mathematicians are, as well as other men, concerned in the errors arising from the doctrine of abstract general ideas, and the existence of objects without the mind.

119. *Arithmetic* has been thought to have for its object abstract ideas of *number*. Of which to understand the properties and mutual habitudes is supposed no mean part of speculative knowledge. The opinion of the pure and intellectual nature of numbers in abstract, has made them in esteem with those philosophers, who seem to have affected an uncommon fineness and elevation of thought. It has set a price on the most trifling numerical speculations which in practice are of no use, but serve only for amusement: and has therefore so far infected the minds of some, that they have dreamt of mighty *mysteries* involved in numbers, and attempted the explication of natural things by them. But if we

inquire into our own thoughts, and consider what has been premised, we may perhaps entertain a low opinion of those high flights and abstractions, and look on all inquiries about numbers, only as so many *difficiles nugae*, so far as they are not subservient to practice, and promote the benefit of life.

120. Unity in abstract we have before considered in *Sect.* 13, from which and what has been said in the Introduction, it plainly follows there is not any such idea. But number being defined a *collection of units*, we may conclude that, if there be no such thing as unity or unit in abstract, there are no ideas of number in abstract denoted by the numeral names and figures. The theories therefore in arithmetic, if they are abstracted from the names and figures, as likewise from all use and practice, as well as from the particular things numbered, can be supposed to have nothing at all for their object. Hence we may see, how entirely the science of numbers is subordinate to practice, and how jejune and trifling it becomes, when considered as a matter of mere speculation.

121. However since there may be some, who, deluded by the specious show of discovering abstracted verities, waste their time in arithmetical theorems and problems, which have not any use: it will not be amiss, if we more fully consider, and expose the vanity of that pretense; and this will plainly appear, by taking a view of arithmetic in its infancy, and observing what it was that originally put men on the study of that science, and to what scope they directed it. It is natural to think that at first, men, for ease of memory and help of computation, made use of counters, or in writing of single strokes, points or the like, each whereof was made to signify a unit, that is, some one thing of whatever kind they had occasion to reckon. Afterwards they found out the more compendious ways, of making one character stand in place of several strokes, or points. And lastly, the notation of the *Arabians* or *Indians* came into use, wherein by the repetition of a few characters or figures, and varying the signification of each figure according to the place it obtains, all numbers may be most aptly expressed: which seems to have been done in imitation of language, so that an exact analogy is observed betwixt the notation by figures, and names, the nine simple figures answering the nine first numeral names, and places in the former corresponding to denominations in the latter.[22] And agreeably to those conditions of the simple and local value of figures, were contrived methods of finding

22. In this sentence I follow the punctuation of the first edition.

from the given figures or marks of the parts, what figures and how placed, are proper to denote the whole or *vice versa*. And having found the sought figures, the same rule or analogy being observed throughout, it is easy to read them into words; and so the number becomes perfectly known. For then the number of any particular things is said to be known, when we know the name or figures (with their due arrangement) that according to the standing analogy belong to them. For these signs being known, we can by the operations of arithmetic, know the signs of any part of the particular sums signified by them; and thus computing in signs, (because of the connection established betwixt them and the distinct multitudes of things, whereof one is taken for a unit,) we may be able rightly to sum up, divide, and proportion the things themselves that we intend to number.

122. In *arithmetic* therefore we regard not the *things* but the *signs*, which nevertheless are not regarded for their own sake, but because they direct us how to act with relation to things, and dispose rightly of them. Now agreeably to what we have before observed, of words in general (*Sect*. 19. *Introd*.) it happens here likewise, that abstract ideas are thought to be signified by numeral names or characters, while they do not suggest ideas of particular things to our minds. I shall not at present enter into a more particular dissertation on this subject; but only observe that it is evident from what has been said, those things which pass for abstract truths and theorems concerning numbers, are, in reality, conversant about no object distinct from particular numerable things, except only names and characters; which originally came to be considered, on no other account but their being *signs*, or capable to represent aptly, whatever particular things men had need to compute. Whence it follows, that to study them for their own sake would be just as wise, and to as good purpose, as if a man, neglecting the true use or original intention and subserviency of language, should spend his time in impertinent criticisms upon words, or reasonings and controversies purely verbal.

123. From numbers we proceed to speak of *extension*, which considered as relative, is the object of geometry. The *infinite* divisibility of *finite* extension, though it is not expressly laid down, either as an axiom or theorem in the elements of that science, yet is throughout the same everywhere supposed, and thought to have so inseparable and essential a connection with the principles and demonstrations in geometry, that mathematicians never admit it into doubt, or make the least question of it. And as this notion is the source from whence do spring all those

amusing geometrical paradoxes, which have such a direct repugnancy to the plain common sense of mankind, and are admitted with so much reluctance into a mind not yet debauched by learning: so is it the principal occasion of all that nice and extreme subtlety, which renders the study of *mathematics* so difficult and tedious. Hence if we can make it appear, that no finite extension contains innumerable parts, or is infinitely divisible, it follows that we shall at once clear the science of geometry from a great number of difficulties and contradictions, which have ever been esteemed a reproach to human reason, and withal make the attainment thereof a business of much less time and pains, than it hitherto has been.

124. Every particular finite extension, which may possibly be the object of our thought, is an *idea* existing only in the mind, and consequently each part thereof must be perceived. If therefore I cannot perceive innumerable parts in any finite extension that I consider, it is certain they are not contained in it: but it is evident, that I cannot distinguish innumerable parts in any particular line, surface, or solid, which I either perceive by sense, or figure to myself in my mind: wherefore I conclude they are not contained in it. Nothing can be plainer to me, than that the extensions I have in view are no other than my own ideas, and it is no less plain, that I cannot resolve any one of my ideas into an infinite number of other ideas, that is, that they are not infinitely divisible. If by *finite extension* be meant something distinct from a finite idea, I declare I do not know what that is, and so cannot affirm or deny anything of it. But if the terms *extension, parts,* and the like, are taken in any sense conceivable, that is, for ideas; then to say a finite quantity or extension consists of parts infinite in number, is so manifest a contradiction, that everyone at first sight acknowledges it to be so. And it is impossible it should ever gain the assent of any reasonable creature, who is not brought to it by gentle and slow degrees, as a converted gentile to the belief of *transubstantiation.*[23] Ancient and rooted prejudices do often pass into principles: and those propositions which once obtain the force and credit of a *principle,* are not only themselves, but likewise whatever is deducible from them, thought privileged from all examination. And there is no absurdity so gross, which by this means the mind of man may not be prepared to swallow.

23. Transubstantiation is the conversion of the substance of the bread and wine of the Eucharist into the substance of the body and blood of Christ.

125. He whose understanding is prepossessed with the doctrine of abstract general ideas, may be persuaded, that (whatever be thought of the ideas of sense,) extension in *abstract* is infinitely divisible. And one who thinks the objects of sense exist without the mind, will perhaps in virtue thereof be brought to admit, that a line but an inch long may contain innumerable parts really existing, though too small to be discerned. These errors are grafted as well in the minds of *geometricians,* as of other men, and have a like influence on their reasonings; and it were no difficult thing, to show how the arguments from geometry made use of to support the infinite divisibility of extension, are bottomed on them. At present we shall only observe in general, whence it is that the mathematicians are all so fond and tenacious of this doctrine.

126. It has been observed in another place, that the theorems and demonstrations in geometry are conversant about universal ideas. *Sect.* 15, *Introd.* Where it is explained in what sense this ought to be understood, to wit, that the particular lines and figures included in the diagram, are supposed to stand for innumerable others of different sizes: or in other words, the geometer considers them abstracting from their magnitude: which does not imply that he forms an abstract idea, but only that he cares not what the particular magnitude is, whether great or small, but looks on that as a thing indifferent to the demonstration: hence it follows, that a line in the scheme, but an inch long, must be spoken of, as though it contained ten thousand parts, since it is regarded not in itself, but as it is universal; and it is universal only in its signification, whereby it represents innumerable lines greater than itself, in which may be distinguished ten thousand parts or more, though there may not be above an inch in it. After this manner the properties of the lines signified are (by a very usual figure) transferred to the sign, and thence through mistake thought to appertain to it considered in its own nature.

127. Because there is no number of parts so great, but it is possible there may be a line containing more, the inch-line is said to contain parts more than any assignable number; which is true, not of the inch taken absolutely, but only for the things signified by it. But men not retaining that distinction in their thoughts, slide into a belief that the small particular line described on paper contains in itself parts innumerable. There is no such thing as the ten-thousandth part of an *inch;* but there is of a *mile* or *diameter of the earth,* which may be signified by that inch. When therefore I delineate a triangle on paper, and take one side not

above an inch, for example, in length to be the *radius:* this I consider as divided into ten thousand or a hundred thousand parts, or more. For though the ten-thousandth part of that line considered in itself, is nothing at all, and consequently may be neglected without any error or inconveniency; yet these described lines being only marks standing for greater quantities, whereof it may be the ten-thousandth part is very considerable, it follows, that to prevent notable errors in practice, the *radius* must be taken of ten thousand parts, or more.

128. From what has been said the reason is plain why, to the end any theorem may become universal in its use, it is necessary we speak of the lines described on paper, as though they contained parts which really they do not. In doing of which, if we examine the matter thoroughly, we shall perhaps discover that we cannot conceive an inch itself as consisting of, or being divisible into a thousand parts, but only some other line which is far greater than an inch, and represented by it. And that when we say a line is *infinitely divisible,* we must mean a line which is *infinitely great.* What we have here observed seems to be the chief cause, why to suppose the infinite divisibility of finite extension has been thought necessary in geometry.

129. The several absurdities and contradictions which flowed from this false principle might, one would think, have been esteemed so many demonstrations against it. But by I know not what *logic,* it is held that proofs *a posteriori* are not to be admitted against propositions relating to infinity. As though it were not impossible even for an infinite mind to reconcile contradictions. Or as if anything absurd and repugnant could have a necessary connection with truth, or flow from it. But whoever considers the weakness of this pretense, will think it was contrived on purpose to humor the laziness of the mind, which had rather acquiesce in an indolent skepticism, than be at the pains to go through with a severe examination of those principles it has ever embraced for true.

130. Of late the speculations about infinites have run so high, and grown to such strange notions, as have occasioned no small scruples and disputes among the geometers of the present age. Some there are of great note, who not content with holding that finite lines may be divided into an infinite number of parts, do yet farther maintain, that each of those infinitesimals is itself subdivisible into an infinity of other parts, or infinitesimals of a second order, and so on *ad infinitum*. These, I say, assert there are infinitesimals of infinitesimals of

infinitesimals, without ever coming to an end. So that according to them an inch does not barely contain an infinite number of parts, but an infinity of an infinity of an infinity *ad infinitum* of parts. Others there be who hold all orders of infinitesimals below the first to be nothing at all, thinking it with good reason absurd, to imagine there is any positive quantity or part of extension, which though multiplied infinitely, can ever equal the smallest given extension.[24] And yet on the other hand it seems no less absurd, to think the square, cube, or other power of a positive real root, should itself be nothing at all; which they who hold infinitesimals of the first order, denying all of the subsequent orders, are obliged to maintain.

131. Have we not therefore reason to conclude, that they are *both* in the wrong, and that there is in effect no such thing as parts infinitely small, or an infinite number of parts contained in any finite quantity? But you will say, that if this doctrine obtains, it will follow the very foundations of geometry are destroyed: and those great men who have raised that science to so astonishing a height, have been all the while building a castle in the air. To this it may be replied, that whatever is useful in geometry and promotes the benefit of human life, does still remain firm and unshaken on our principles. That science considered as practical, will rather receive advantage than any prejudice from what has been said. But to set this in a due light, may be the subject of a distinct inquiry. For the rest, though it should follow that some of the more intricate and subtle parts of *speculative mathematics* may be pared off without any prejudice to truth; yet I do not see what damage will be thence derived to mankind. On the contrary, it were highly to be wished, that men of great abilities and obstinate application would draw off their thoughts from those amusements, and employ them in the study of such things as lie nearer the concerns of life, or have a more direct influence on the manners.

132. If it be said that several theorems undoubtedly true, are discovered by methods in which infinitesimals are made use of, which could never have been, if their existence included a contradiction in it. I answer, that upon a thorough examination it will not be found, that in any instance it is necessary to make use of or conceive infinitesimal parts of finite lines,

---

24. The first edition has "can never equal" where the second edition has "can ever equal." The first edition is probably correct; its wording matches a parallel passage at *Analyst* 5.

or even quantities less than the *minimum sensibile:* nay, it will be evident this is never done, it being impossible.[25]

133. By what we have premised, it is plain that very numerous and important errors have taken their rise from those false principles, which were impugned in the foregoing parts of this treatise. And the opposites of those erroneous tenets at the same time appear to be most fruitful principles, from whence do flow innumerable consequences highly advantageous to true philosophy as well as to religion. Particularly, *matter* or *the absolute existence of corporeal objects*, has been shown to be that wherein the most avowed and pernicious enemies of all knowledge, whether human or divine, have ever placed their chief strength and confidence. And surely, if by distinguishing the real existence of unthinking things from their being perceived, and allowing them a subsistence of their own out of the minds of spirits, no one thing is explained in nature; but on the contrary a great many inexplicable difficulties arise: if the supposition of matter is barely precarious, as not being grounded on so much as one single reason: if its consequences cannot endure the light of examination and free inquiry, but screen themselves under the dark and general pretense of *infinites being incomprehensible:* if withal the removal of this *matter* be not attended with the least evil consequence, if it be not even missed in the world, but everything as well, nay much easier conceived without it: if lastly, both *skeptics* and *atheists* are forever silenced upon supposing only spirits and ideas, and this scheme of things is perfectly agreeable both to *reason* and *religion:* methinks we may expect it should be admitted and firmly embraced, though it were proposed only as a *hypothesis*, and the existence of matter had been allowed possible, which yet I think we have evidently demonstrated that it is not.

134. True it is, that in consequence of the foregoing principles, several disputes and speculations, which are esteemed no mean parts of learning, are rejected as useless. But how great a prejudice soever against our notions, this may give to those who have already been deeply engaged, and made large advances in studies of that nature: yet by others, we hope it will not be thought any just ground of dislike to the principles and tenets herein laid down, that they abridge the labor of study, and

25. The *minimum sensibile* is the smallest quantity capable of being sensed, a "sensible point." Berkeley discusses the *minima sensibilia* of sight and touch at *Theory of Vision* 54 and 80–83.

make human sciences more clear, compendious, and attainable, than they were before.

135. Having dispatched what we intended to say concerning the knowledge of *ideas,* the method we proposed leads us, in the next place, to treat of *spirits:* with regard to which, perhaps human knowledge is not so deficient as is vulgarly imagined. The great reason that is assigned for our being thought ignorant of the nature of spirits, is, our not having an idea of it. But surely it ought not to be looked on as a defect in a human understanding, that it does not perceive the idea of *spirit,* if it is manifestly impossible there should be any such *idea.* And this, if I mistake not, has been demonstrated in *Sect.* 27: to which I shall here add that a spirit has been shown to be the only substance or support, wherein the unthinking beings or ideas can exist: but that this *substance* which supports or perceives ideas should itself be an *idea* or like an *idea,* is evidently absurd.

136. It will perhaps be said, that we want a sense (as some have imagined) proper to know substances withal, which if we had, we might know our own soul, as we do a triangle. To this I answer, that in case we had a new sense bestowed upon us, we could only receive thereby some new sensations or ideas of sense. But I believe nobody will say, that what he means by the terms *soul* and *substance,* is only some particular sort of idea or sensation. We may therefore infer, that all things duly considered, it is not more reasonable to think our faculties defective, in that they do not furnish us with an idea of spirit or active thinking substance, than it would be if we should blame them for not being able to comprehend a *round square.*

137. From the opinion that spirits are to be known after the manner of an idea or sensation, have risen many absurd and heterodox tenets, and much skepticism about the nature of the soul. It is even probable, that this opinion may have produced a doubt in some, whether they had any soul at all distinct from their body, since upon inquiry they could not find they had an idea of it. That an *idea* which is inactive, and the existence whereof consists in being perceived, should be the image or likeness of an agent subsisting by itself, seems to need no other refutation, than barely attending to what is meant by those words. But perhaps you will say, that though an *idea* cannot resemble a *spirit,* in its thinking, acting, or subsisting by itself, yet it may in some other respects: and it is not necessary that an idea or image be in all respects like the original.

138. I answer, if it does not in those mentioned, it is impossible it should represent it in any other thing. Do but leave out the power of willing, thinking, and perceiving ideas, and there remains nothing else wherein the idea can be like a spirit. For by the word *spirit* we mean only that which thinks, wills, and perceives; this, and this alone, constitutes the signification of that term. If therefore it is impossible that any degree of those powers should be represented in an idea, it is evident there can be no idea of a spirit.[26]

139. But it will be objected, that if there is no idea signified by the terms *soul, spirit*, and *substance*, they are wholly insignificant, or have no meaning in them. I answer, those words do mean or signify a real thing, which is neither an idea nor like an idea, but that which perceives ideas, and wills, and reasons about them. What I am myself, that which I denote by the term I, is the same with what is meant by *soul* or *spiritual substance*.[27] If it be said that this is only quarrelling at a word, and that since the immediate significations of other names are by common consent called *ideas*, no reason can be assigned, why that which is signified by the name *spirit* or *soul* may not partake in the same appellation. I answer, all the unthinking objects of the mind agree, in that they are entirely passive, and their existence consists only in being perceived: whereas a soul or spirit is an active being, whose existence consists not in being perceived, but in perceiving ideas and thinking. It is therefore necessary, in order to prevent equivocation and confounding natures perfectly disagreeing and unlike, that we distinguish between *spirit* and *idea*. See *Sect.* 27.

140. In a large sense indeed, we may be said to have an idea, or rather a notion of *spirit*, that is, we understand the meaning of the word, otherwise we could not affirm or deny anything of it.[28] Moreover, as we conceive the ideas that are in the minds of other spirits by means of our own, which we suppose to be resemblances of them: so we know other spirits by means of our own soul, which in that sense is the image or idea of them, it having a like respect to other spirits, that blueness or heat by me perceived has to those ideas perceived by another.

26. In this sentence in the first edition, the words "or notion" follow each appearance of "idea."

27. In the first edition, the following sentence is inserted here: *But if I should say, that I was nothing, or that I was an idea or notion, nothing could be more evidently absurd than either of these propositions.*

28. The words "or rather a notion" were added in the second edition.

141. It must not be supposed, that they who assert the natural immortality of the soul are of opinion, that it is absolutely incapable of annihilation even by the infinite power of the Creator who first gave it being: but only that it is not liable to be broken or dissolved by the ordinary laws of nature or motion. They indeed, who hold the soul of man to be only a thin vital flame, or system of animal spirits, make it perishing and corruptible as the body, since there is nothing more easily dissipated than such a being, which it is naturally impossible should survive the ruin of the tabernacle, wherein it is enclosed. And this notion has been greedily embraced and cherished by the worst part of mankind, as the most effectual antidote against all impressions of virtue and religion. But it has been made evident, that bodies of what frame or texture soever, are barely passive ideas in the mind, which is more distant and heterogeneous from them, than light is from darkness. We have shown that the soul is indivisible, incorporeal, unextended, and it is consequently incorruptible. Nothing can be plainer, than that the motions, changes, decays, and dissolutions which we hourly see befall natural bodies (and which is what we mean by the *course of nature*) cannot possibly affect an active, simple, uncompounded substance: such a being therefore is indissoluble by the force of nature, that is to say, *the soul of man is naturally immortal.*

142. After what has been said, it is I suppose plain, that our souls are not to be known in the same manner as senseless inactive objects, or by way of *idea. Spirits* and *ideas* are things so wholly different, that when we say, *they exist, they are known,* or the like, these words must not be thought to signify anything common to both natures. There is nothing alike or common in them: and to expect that by any multiplication or enlargement of our faculties, we may be enabled to know a spirit as we do a triangle, seems as absurd as if we should hope to *see a sound.* This is inculcated because I imagine it may be of moment towards clearing several important questions, and preventing some very dangerous errors concerning the nature of the soul. [We may not I think strictly be said to have an idea of an active being, or of an action, although we may be said to have a notion of them. I have some knowledge or notion of my mind, and its acts about ideas, inasmuch as I know or understand what is meant by those words. What I know, that I have some notion of. I will not say, that the terms *idea* and *notion* may not be used convertibly, if the world will have it so. But yet it conduces to clearness and propriety, that we distinguish things very different by different names. It is also to be

remarked, that all relations including an act of the mind, we cannot so properly be said to have an idea, but rather a notion of the relations or habitudes between things. But if in the modern way the word *idea* is extended to spirits, and relations and acts; this is after all an affair of verbal concern.][29]

143. It will not be amiss to add, that the doctrine of *abstract ideas* has had no small share in rendering those sciences intricate and obscure, which are particularly conversant about spiritual things. Men have imagined they could frame abstract notions of the powers and acts of the mind, and consider them prescinded, as well from the mind or spirit itself, as from their respective objects and effects. Hence a great number of dark and ambiguous terms presumed to stand for abstract notions, have been introduced into metaphysics and morality, and from these have grown infinite distractions and disputes amongst the learned.

144. But nothing seems more to have contributed towards engaging men in controversies and mistakes, with regard to the nature and operations of the mind, than the being used to speak of those things, in terms borrowed from sensible ideas. For example, the will is termed the *motion* of the soul: this infuses a belief, that the mind of man is as a ball in motion, impelled and determined by the objects of sense, as necessarily as that is by the stroke of a racket.[30] Hence arise endless scruples and errors of dangerous consequence in morality. All which I doubt not may be cleared, and truth appear plain, uniform, and consistent, could but philosophers be prevailed on to retire into themselves, and attentively consider their own meaning.

145. From what has been said, it is plain that we cannot know the existence of other spirits, otherwise than by their operations, or the ideas by them excited in us. I perceive several motions, changes, and combinations of ideas, that inform me there are certain particular agents like myself, which accompany them, and concur in their production. Hence the knowledge I have of other spirits is not immediate, as is the knowledge of my ideas: but depending on the intervention of ideas, by me referred to agents or spirits distinct from myself, as effects or concomitant signs.

29. The bracketed passage was added in the second edition.

30. Berkeley is apparently thinking of Hobbes. At *Philosophical Commentaries* 822 he writes that it is "Silly of Hobbs etc to speak of ye Will as if it were Motion."

146. But though there be some things which convince us, human agents are concerned in producing them; yet it is evident to everyone, that those things which are called the works of nature, that is, the far greater part of the ideas or sensations perceived by us, are not produced by, or dependent on the wills of men. There is therefore some other spirit that causes them, since it is repugnant that they should subsist by themselves. See *Sect.* 29. But if we attentively consider the constant regularity, order, and concatenation of natural things, the surprising magnificence, beauty, and perfection of the larger, and the exquisite contrivance of the smaller parts of the creation, together with the exact harmony and correspondence of the whole, but above all, the never enough admired laws of pain and pleasure, and the instincts or natural inclinations, appetites, and passions of animals; I say if we consider all these things, and at the same time attend to the meaning and import of the attributes, one, eternal, infinitely wise, good, and perfect, we shall clearly perceive that they belong to the aforesaid spirit, *who works all in all*, and *by whom all things consist*.[31]

147. Hence it is evident, that God is known as certainly and immediately as any other mind or spirit whatsoever, distinct from ourselves. We may even assert, that the existence of God is far more evidently perceived than the existence of men; because the effects of nature are infinitely more numerous and considerable, than those ascribed to human agents. There is not any one mark that denotes a man, or effect produced by him, which does not more strongly evince the being of that spirit who is the *Author of Nature*. For it is evident that in affecting other persons, the will of man has no other object, than barely the motion of the limbs of his body; but that such a motion should be attended by, or excite any idea in the mind of another, depends wholly on the will of the Creator. He alone it is who *upholding all things by the word of his power*, maintains that intercourse between spirits, whereby they are able to perceive the existence of each other.[32] And yet this pure and clear light which enlightens everyone, is itself invisible.

148. It seems to be a general pretense of the unthinking herd, that they cannot see God. Could we but see him, say they, as we see a man, we should believe that he is, and believing obey his commands. But alas we need only open our eyes to see the sovereign lord of all things with a

31. *who works all in all*, 1 Corinthians 12:6; *by whom all things consist*, Colossians 1:17.

32. *upholding all things by . . . his power*, Hebrews 1:3.

more full and clear view, than we do any one of our fellow-creatures. Not that I imagine we see God (as some will have it) by a direct and immediate view, or see corporeal things, not by themselves, but by seeing that which represents them in the essence of God, which doctrine is I must confess to me incomprehensible.[33] But I shall explain my meaning. A human spirit or person is not perceived by sense, as not being an idea; when therefore we see the color, size, figure, and motions of a man, we perceive only certain sensations or ideas excited in our own minds: and these being exhibited to our view in sundry distinct collections, serve to mark out unto us the existence of finite and created spirits like ourselves. Hence it is plain, we do not see a man, if by *man* is meant that which lives, moves, perceives, and thinks as we do: but only such a certain collection of ideas, as directs us to think there is a distinct principle of thought and motion like to ourselves, accompanying and represented by it. And after the same manner we see God; all the difference is, that whereas some one finite and narrow assemblage of ideas denotes a particular human mind, whithersoever we direct our view, we do at all times and in all places perceive manifest tokens of the Divinity: everything we see, hear, feel, or any wise perceive by sense, being a sign or effect of the power of God; as is our perception of those very motions, which are produced by men.

149. It is therefore plain, that nothing can be more evident to anyone that is capable of the least reflection, than the existence of God, or a spirit who is intimately present to our minds, producing in them all that variety of ideas or sensations, which continually affect us, on whom we have an absolute and entire dependence, in short, *in whom we live, and move, and have our being.*[34] That the discovery of this great truth which lies so near and obvious to the mind, should be attained to by the reason of so very few, is a sad instance of the stupidity and inattention of men, who, though they are surrounded with such clear manifestations of the Deity, are yet so little affected by them, that they seem as it were blinded with excess of light.

150. But you will say, has nature no share in the production of natural things, and must they be all ascribed to the immediate and sole operation

---

33. Malebranche believes that "we see all things in God." See *The Search after Truth,* Book 3, Part 2, chapter 6. Berkeley explains how he differs from Malebranche in *Three Dialogues* 2 (*Works* II, pp. 213–15; Adams, pp. 48–50).

34. Acts 17:28.

of God? I answer, if by *nature* is meant only the visible *series* of effects, or sensations imprinted on our minds according to certain fixed and general laws: then it is plain, that nature taken in this sense cannot produce anything at all. But if by *nature* is meant some being distinct from God, as well as from the laws of nature, and things perceived by sense, I must confess that word is to me an empty sound, without any intelligible meaning annexed to it. Nature in this acceptation is a vain *chimera* introduced by those heathens, who had not just notions of the omnipresence and infinite perfection of God. But it is more unaccountable, that it should be received among *Christians* professing belief in the Holy Scriptures, which constantly ascribe those effects to the immediate hand of God, that heathen philosophers are wont to impute to *nature*. *The Lord, he causeth the vapors to ascend; he maketh lightnings with rain; he bringeth forth the wind out of his treasures,* Jerem. Chap. 10. ver. 13. *He turneth the shadow of death into the morning, and maketh the day dark with night,* Amos Chap. 5. ver. 8. *He visiteth the earth, and maketh it soft with showers: he blesseth the springing thereof, and crowneth the year with his goodness; so that the pastures are clothed with flocks, and the valleys are covered over with corn.* See *Psalm* 65. But notwithstanding that this is the constant language of Scripture; yet we have I know not what aversion from believing, that God concerns himself so nearly in our affairs. Fain would we suppose him at a great distance off, and substitute some blind unthinking deputy in his stead, though (if we may believe Saint *Paul*) he be not far from every one of us.[35]

151. It will I doubt not be objected, that the slow and gradual methods observed in the production of natural things, do not seem to have for their cause the immediate hand of an *almighty agent*. Besides, monsters, untimely births, fruits blasted in the blossom, rains falling in desert places, miseries incident to human life, are so many arguments that the whole frame of nature is not immediately actuated and superintended by a spirit of infinite wisdom and goodness. But the answer to this objection is in a good measure plain from *Sect.* 62, it being visible, that the aforesaid methods of nature are absolutely necessary, in order to working by the most simple and general rules, and after a steady and consistent manner; which argues both the *wisdom* and *goodness* of God. Such is the artificial contrivance of this mighty machine of nature, that whilst its motions and various phenomena strike on our senses, the hand which actuates the whole is itself unperceivable to men of flesh and

35. Acts 17:27.

blood. *Verily* (says the prophet) *thou art a God that hidest thyself,* Isaiah Chap. 45. ver. 15. But though God conceal himself from the eyes of the *sensual* and *lazy,* who will not be at the least expense of thought; yet to an unbiased and attentive mind, nothing can be more plainly legible, than the intimate presence of an *all-wise spirit,* who fashions, regulates, and sustains the whole system of being. It is clear from what we have elsewhere observed, that the operating according to general and stated laws, is so necessary for our guidance in the affairs of life, and letting us into the secret of nature, that without it, all reach and compass of thought, all human sagacity and design could serve to no manner of purpose: it were even impossible there should be any such faculties or powers in the mind. See *Sect.* 31. Which one consideration abundantly out-balances whatever particular inconveniences may thence arise.

152. We should further consider, that the very blemishes and defects of nature are not without their use, in that they make an agreeable sort of variety, and augment the beauty of the rest of the creation, as shades in a picture serve to set off the brighter and more enlightened parts. We would likewise do well to examine, whether our taxing the waste of seeds and embryos, and accidental destruction of plants and animals, before they come to full maturity, as an imprudence in the Author of Nature, be not the effect of prejudice contracted by our familiarity with impotent and saving mortals. In *man* indeed a thrifty management of those things, which he cannot procure without much pains and industry, may be esteemed *wisdom.* But we must not imagine, that the inexplicably fine machines of an animal or vegetable, costs the great Creator any more pains or trouble in its production than a pebble does: nothing being more evident, than that an omnipotent spirit can indifferently produce everything by a mere *fiat* or act of his will. Hence it is plain, that the splendid profusion of natural things should not be interpreted, weakness or prodigality in the agent who produces them, but rather be looked on as an argument of the riches of his power.

153. As for the mixture of pain or uneasiness which is in the world, pursuant to the general laws of nature, and the actions of finite imperfect spirits: this, in the state we are in at present, is indispensably necessary to our well-being. But our prospects are too narrow: we take, for instance, the idea of some one particular pain into our thoughts, and account it *evil;* whereas if we enlarge our view, so as to comprehend the various ends, connections, and dependencies of things, on what occasions and in what proportions we are affected with pain and

pleasure, the nature of human freedom, and the design with which we are put into the world; we shall be forced to acknowledge that those particular things, which considered in themselves appear to be *evil*, have the nature of *good*, when considered as linked with the whole system of beings.

154. From what has been said it will be manifest to any considering person, that it is merely for want of attention and comprehensiveness of mind, that there are any favorers of *atheism* or the *Manichean heresy* to be found.[36] Little and unreflecting souls may indeed burlesque the works of providence, the beauty and order whereof they have not capacity, or will not be at the pains to comprehend. But those who are masters of any justness and extent of thought, and are withal used to reflect, can never sufficiently admire the divine traces of wisdom and goodness that shine throughout the economy of nature. But what truth is there which shines so strongly on the mind, that by an aversion of thought, a willful shutting of the eyes, we may not escape seeing it? Is it therefore to be wondered at, if the generality of men, who are ever intent on business or pleasure, and little used to fix or open the eye of their mind, should not have all that conviction and evidence of the being of God, which might be expected in reasonable creatures?

155. We should rather wonder, that men can be found so stupid as to neglect, than that neglecting they should be unconvinced of such an evident and momentous truth. And yet it is to be feared that too many of parts and leisure, who live in Christian countries, are merely through a supine and dreadful negligence sunk into a sort of *atheism*. Since it is downright impossible, that a soul pierced and enlightened with a thorough sense of the omnipresence, holiness, and justice of that *Almighty Spirit*, should persist in a remorseless violation of his laws. We ought therefore earnestly to meditate and dwell on those important points; that so we may attain conviction without all scruple, *that the eyes of the Lord are in every place beholding the evil and the good; that he is with us and keepeth us in all places whither we go, and giveth us bread to eat, and raiment to put on;* that he is present and conscious to our innermost thoughts; and that we have a most absolute and immediate dependence on him.[37] A

36. The Manicheans (followers of Mani, c. 216–276) believed that the world is governed by two competing principles, one good, the other evil.

37. *that the eyes are . . . beholding the evil and the good,* Proverbs 15:3; *that he is with us . . . and giveth us . . . raiment to put on,* Genesis 28:20.

clear view of which great truths cannot choose but fill our hearts with an awful circumspection and holy fear, which is the strongest incentive to *virtue*, and the best guard against *vice*.

156. For after all, what deserves the first place in our studies, is the consideration of *God*, and our *duty;* which to promote, as it was the main drift and design of my labors, so shall I esteem them altogether useless and ineffectual, if by what I have said I cannot inspire my readers with a pious sense of the presence of God: and having shown the falseness or vanity of those barren speculations, which make the chief employment of learned men, the better dispose them to reverence and embrace the salutary truths of the Gospel, which to know and to practice is the highest perfection of human nature.

Glossary

This list includes archaic words, words used in archaic senses, technical terms, foreign expressions not explained in the notes, and other words which may be unfamiliar to the twentieth-century reader. Berkeley uses many of the items listed in both familiar and unfamiliar senses, but only unfamiliar senses are presented. In preparing the glossary I consulted both the *Oxford English Dictionary* and Samuel Johnson's *A Dictionary of the English Language*.

absolute independent *(as in section 3)*, complete *(as in section 149)*

acceptation received meaning

accident quality, attribute

ad infinitum "to infinity," without limit

affection quality, attribute

agreement *(as in Introduction 9)* (a point of) similarity or likeness

ambient surrounding

amuse beguile, distract, engage

antipodes people or places on the other side of the globe

appellation name

apposite proper, fit

archetype original pattern or model

attraction power by which a thing is drawn, gravity

aught anything

awful *(as in section 155)* filled with awe

banter *(as in section 101)* bamboozle

barely merely, simply, only

bent turn, inclination

betwixt between

blast wither, shrivel, blight

caviller one who makes picky or frivolous objections

cheap easy to be had

chimera a creature of the imagination, something unreal

choir *(as in "choir of the planets")* organized collection

clear (verb) explain, clarify

collect gather, conclude, infer

color *(as in section 35)* cloak, pretext

common *(as in Introduction 9)* shared

compages structure, framework

comprehend *(as in Introduction 18)* contain

confutation disproof

consistence consistency, texture

contrivance *(as in section 63)* artifice

convertibly interchangeably

corporeal material

corpuscle particle of matter, atom

countenance (noun)   support, encouragement

counter (noun)   a piece of metal or stone used in reckoning

credit (noun)   credibility, right to be believed, repute

curvilinear   curved

debauched   corrupted

deliver   relate, communicate

denominate   name, *but in section 28,* give the right to be called, constitute

depreciate   undervalue

derogate   take away, detract

difficiles nugae   bothersome trifles

dilate   enlarge (on a topic)

discover   disclose

dispose   (as in section 122) employ, turn to a particular end

divers (adjective)   several, various

divine (noun)   theologian

dreadful   to be feared

efficient cause   agent of change *(see the Editor's Introduction, p. xxvii)*

embarras (noun)   embarrassment, perplexity

embarrassment   perplexity

embrangle   entangle, confuse

entire   complete, total

entity   thing, *but in section 99,* existence

entrails   interior

entreat   ask

equicrural   of a triangle: having legs of equal size, isosceles

esteem (verb)   judge

extension   size, or the property of occupying space

faculty   power

fain (adverb)   gladly

fatalism   the doctrine that everything happens by necessity

fiat   command

final cause   the end or goal of change *(see the Editor's Introduction, p. xxvii)*

fine   refined, subtle

forthwith   at once

frame   make, imagine

furniture   (as in "furniture of the earth") contents

genius   character, spirit

gravel   perplex, puzzle

gross   palpable, evident

habitude   relation

handle   something of which use is made or advantage taken

hitherto   up to now

impertinent   irrelevant

impressed force   force exerted on a body by another body

incommunicable   (as in section 117) incapable of being shared

inert   inactive

infinitesimal (noun)   infinitely small quantity

ingenuous   open, fair

jejune   empty, barren

just   exact, true

let (noun)   obstacle

manners way of life, behavior

materialist one who believes in matter or material substance

mean (adjective) unimportant

mechanical cause a cause that operates by impact

meridian the line the sun crosses at noon

methinks it seems to me, I think

mode quality, attribute

mundane belonging to the world or cosmos

narrow close, precise, careful

never so ever so

nice close, careful, *but in section 5,* refined, subtle

numberless innumerable

obliquangular of a triangle: not right-angled

oblique of a triangle: not right-angled

obtuse dull, not acute

occasion (when contrasted with cause) event that accompanies a cause *(see section 69)*

occult quality hidden cause of a manifest effect

ought (variant of aught) anything

parts abilities, talents

peculiar singular

perfect (as in Introduction 17) complete, utter

prate talk, chatter

prepossessed filled (with an opinion), biased

prescind cut off

professor one who makes an open declaration of belief or allegiance

prognostic omen, indication

prolix long, tedious

proportionably in proportion

propriety fitness

prospect view (especially of the future)

providence wise arrangement or management; "inspection of a superior mind over the affairs of the world" *(section 93)*

quiddity essence

quiescent motionless, inactive

quit give up

reach (noun) extent

rectangle (adjective) of a triangle: right-angled

rectilinear straight

reflection the mind's notice of its own self

sapid having taste or flavor

scalenon of a triangle: scalene, having three unequal sides

scruple (noun) doubt, hesitation

scrupulous careful

second cause a cause intermediate between God (the "first cause") and a natural event, natural cause

senseless (as in section 9) void of perception or feeling

since (as in section 43) ago

somewhat (noun) something

sound (verb) investigate

speculative theoretical

stay delay, obstruct

strangely *(section 4)* very greatly

stress weightiness, point

substratum that which underlies the qualities of a thing, substance

subsist exist

supine thoughtless, careless, indolent

sustentation sustenance

tax censure

terraqueous composed of land and water

thus much so much

tolerable able to be endured or supported, passable; *in the context of section 60*, reasonable

transcendental general

translation motion

unaccountable inexplicable

uncouth strange, unusual

vain empty, idle, false

verity truth

vide see, refer to

vitiate to spoil or pervert, leading to false judgments or preferences

vulgar common, ordinary

want (verb) need, lack

whilst while

withal *(as in Introduction 19)* at the same time, likewise; *(as in section 136)* with

without *(as in "without the mind")* outside

wont (adjective) in "wont to be," accustomed to being, in the habit of being

wonted customary, usual

Index

absolute existence of objects without the mind, 23, 27, 32, 58, 77

abstract ideas, xiii–xxi, xxxiv, 8–20, 24–25, 27–28, 54, 61–62, 66–67, 69, 70, 72, 74, 81; impossibility of, xv–xvi, xix, 19; language as source of belief in, 17, 19; and materialism, xxxiv–xxxv, 24; of things, 9–11; of qualities, xx–xxi, 9–11, 12; *see also* abstraction

abstraction: contrasted with consideration, xviii, xix, 16; in the strict sense, xv–xvi, xviii, 25; twofold, 62; *see also* abstract ideas

absurdity, 8, 40, 49, 73, 75–76

accidents, 28–29, 51, 52; absurdity of substance without, 49, 54; absurdity of, without substance, 49; relation of subject to, 42; *see also* mode; qualities

action, no idea of, 80–81

active being, *see* spirit

activity, agency, xxvi–xxviii, 32–33, 35, 45, 47, 63

algebra, 18

alone in the world without language, xii

analogy, 64, 65–66, 71

animals, parts of, 46–49

antipodes, 44

appearances, 47, 51, 57, 63

Aquinas, Thomas, 16*n*

archetypes, 26, 57, 58; can exist only in another mind, 62

argument: *ad hominem*, xviii; *a posteriori*, 31, 75; *a priori*, 31, 46

Aristotle, xxvii, 16*n*, 19, 27

arithmetic, 70–72

astronomers, astronomy, 45–46

atheism, atheists, 36, 59, 60, 77, 86

atoms, *see* particles

attention, 20, 32, 33; selective, xviii–xix, 16

attraction, 63–64

attributes, *see* accidents; mode; qualities

attribution, and inherence,xxv–xxvi, 41–42

Author of Nature, *see* God

bachelor, married, taken as example, xvi–xvii

Bayle, Pierre, xxix*n*

being, 57; in general, idea of, 33, 52

Bible, *see* Scripture

blind, man born, 39, 53

body, 40, 63, 68–69, 80; being of, is to be perceived or known, 25; external, 29–32; meaning of, xxx, 60; no reason to suppose existence of, 29–30; one's own, 36, 39, 82

books, in a closet, taken as example, 31

Boyle, Robert, xxviii

Cana, 55

cause, xxi, xxiv, xxvi–xxviii, xxxi, 63; corporeal, 45, 49; and effect, xxiii, xxiv, xxviii; efficient, xxvii–xxviii, 43, 63, 64, 65; and explanation, xxiv, xxvi–xxvii; final, xxvii–xviii, 46, 65; mechanical, 63; natural, taken away, 42; second, 35; contrasted with sign, 48–49, 65

chance, 59

chimeras, 35–36, 55, 84

Christ, 55

Christian, 55, 60, 84, 86

color, xxiii, xxiv, 23, 25, 28, 31, 51, 57, 62, 63; abstract ideas of, 9–10

common sense, 7, 11, 68, 73

communication, xiii, 13–14, 18; not the only end of language, 18

comparison, of idea to thing, xxiv

comprehension, scantiness of, 54

conceivability, 20, 25, 26–27, 73; coincides with possibility, xv–xvi, xxxiv; *see also* conceive

conceive, xv, xvii–xx, 11, 13, 20, 24–27, 31–32, 36, 40, 66, 75, 77; *see also* conceivability

concurrence, of mankind, a weak argument for truth, 44

93